RIKKI & ME

RIKKI & ME

KATE FULTON

BLACK & WHITE PUBLISHING

First published 2004
by Black & White Publishing Ltd
99 Giles Street, Edinburgh, Scotland

Reprinted 2004

ISBN 1 84502 003 0

British Library Cataloguing in Publication Data:
A catalogue record for this book is available
from the British Library.

Photograph credits:
The author would like to thank: Pat Morris for the
photograph of Jake, Trinity Mirror Group, Martin Shields
and the *Evening Times*, and Mark Gudgeon for their kindness
in supplying many of the photographs included here.

Cover design: www.henrysteadman.com

Printed and bound by ScandBook AB

CONTENTS

ACKNOWLEDGEMENTS

My thanks to my great nephew Ross Caldwell for
teaching me how to use my computer without
ever losing his temper! He is a *great* nephew.

And my thanks to Tony Roper for his wisdom,
advice and humour, and to his lovely wife
Isobel for her encouragement.

And to my friend and hairdresser, Jim Whitson,
for putting up with me every week, on good days
or bad, and for making me laugh.

And most of all my eternal thanks to Rikki
for being with me. He was the love of my life,
he still is and always will be.

DEDICATION

To everyone who enjoyed Rikki's entertainment
and gave him so much pleasure by their response

PROLOGUE

Rikki's autobiography *Is it that time already?* was published in time for his 75th birthday. For most people, three quarters of a century is one of life's big milestones, but not for Rikki! He just shrugged it off. And he could never *ever* remember birthdays or anniversaries.

One of our favourite restaurants in Glasgow was Rogano, and I can't tell you how often we were there with Rikki saying, 'Why are we here tonight?'

'Because it's your birthday, darling.'

'Oh, is it?' he'd say with a complete lack of interest, going straight back to his Dover sole.

A couple of years later, Rikki's publishers felt that they would like to mark Rikki's next big birthday with some sort of tribute, perhaps a celebration of Rikki's career and asked me if I would think about doing something, maybe a collection of press cuttings, photographs and anecdotes. But I wasn't too keen – I felt there wasn't enough new material there to add to what Rikki had already written in his book – but I said I would think carefully about it and see if I could come up with something. Then our dear friend Tony Roper said, 'Why don't you write a book about him? After all no one knows him better than you.' Which, of course, was quite true.

1

CURTAIN UP

I was fourteen when I met Rikki Fulton and I knew straight away that he was the man I wanted to share my life with.

Rikki was appearing in Noel Coward's *Hayfever* with the Giffnock Theatre Players in Glasgow and my father, a keen amateur actor, was the company's Vice-Chairman. When I came home from school on vacation he took me to see their latest production and when the actor playing the diplomat made his entrance, walked purposefully across the stage, tapped the barometer which then fell to the floor, the audience roared with laughter. They generally did at Rikki Fulton.

I didn't.

I sat there mesmerised.

It was, quite simply, love at first sight. The fact that he was married and I was fourteen were admittedly obstacles, but I could dream, couldn't I?

In the school holidays I would take our Scottie for walks in the woods opposite our house, and there I would go to my 'Wishing Tree'. It was a lovely tree, with one branch that stretched across a burn. I used to climb on to this branch and make a wish, and it was quite incredible how often these wishes came true. I would sit on my branch for ages, with my eyes tight shut, wishing with all my heart that some day, somehow, I could be with Rikki Fulton; but in my heart of hearts, even I knew that it was pretty unlikely.

In those early days Rikki, and everyone else, knew me as Audrey Matheson Craig-Brown – can you wonder that I later changed it? – and my family and I lived in Newton Mearns on the south side of Glasgow. It was there that I fell in love with Sunday school and at the age of four announced that when I grew up I was going to be a minister. I was very gently told that in those days there really wasn't a future for women in the Church.

That was a real blow. However, undaunted, at the age of five, I had the answer. Gathering the family together I told them that if I couldn't be a minister, I would be an actress! Considering that at the time I wore steel-rimmed glasses, was seriously lacking in teeth and had a pronounced lisp, the chances of success in my chosen profession seemed remote, but my parents were too kind to point this out.

For myself, I felt as though a great weight had been lifted from my shoulders. I had made my decision, I now knew where my future lay and I could get on with my life.

My education began and very nearly ended at Hutcheson's Girls Grammar School, or 'Hutchie' as it is affectionately known. I think I was an average pupil, though I was considered rather good at hockey, mainly because I tended to go for the shins!

My other memory of Hutchie was being expelled from the Domestic Science class. The room was arranged in a horseshoe shape, and we each had our own baking boards. One day we were told to make scones, but having made the dough I became very bored. My best friend Bud was right opposite me, and to relieve the boredom I threw my scone dough at her. Unfortunately the Domestic Science teacher walked into the horseshoe just at that moment and got it full in the face! That was the end of my domesticity. It was also the end of my time at Hutchie.

My parents had asked Doreen, my elder sister, if she would like to go to boarding school, but she preferred to stay at home. When I was given the same choice I started to pack straight away! I loved my parents dearly, but I could never resist trying something new, and anyway, I had read all the Angela Brazil books.

My next school made St Trinian's look like Cheltenham Ladies' College.

It was St Marie's and was in Kilbryde Castle near Dunblane. I had the most wonderful time there, though it was sadly lacking in education. To give you an example, our so-called science lab was in a cottage in the grounds, and quite inadvertently, I promise you, during an experiment we blew a hole in the roof. Our Principal, Mrs Dunsmuir, was totally unfazed when she was told that science would have to come off the curriculum. 'Oh, never mind,' she said, 'we'll teach them bridge instead, it will be much more useful.'

Mrs Dunsmuir was an astonishing person. She had no qualifications whatsoever, apart from an LRAM in music. I always thought that she didn't walk, she sailed, like a battleship, and she was built rather like one. She had nails like talons, always painted scarlet, and she wore very heavy make-up, lips bright red, and loads of eye shadow and mascara, topped by a very obvious wig. In spite of all that, the parents were totally in awe of her, and at sports day you could hear the mothers saying, with some envy, 'She is so beautifully corseted.'

She really was more like a monarch than a principal; we had to curtsey to her every time we met.

My favourite subjects were English and French, and I was so lucky that English was taught by our excellent Headmistress, the only member of staff who knew what she was doing. Apart, that is, from an ogre of a Matron who lined up the whole school, all 56 of us, after breakfast, and dosed us with cod liver oil. If there is one thing I cannot cope with, it's oil in any shape or form. We were allowed to write one letter home each week, but it had to be censored by Mrs Dunsmuir, whose only interest was fees. My first letter home explained to my parents about the oil, and how it made me violently ill, and that if it didn't stop, then I would have to leave St Marie's. The following day Matron told me that she had decided that Parish's Chemical Food would be better for me, and so it was, with not a trace of oil!

As I said, my other favourite subject was French, and that was taught by Mr Conrad, an Anglican priest who also taught maths, which I loathed.

One day he called me into the staff room and said, 'Audrey, your maths is appalling – what are you going to do about it?'

I said comfortingly, 'Please don't worry Mr Conrad, I just don't have a mathematical brain, and I won't need maths in my career.'

'And what, pray, is your chosen profession?'

'I'm going to be an actress.'

Mr Conrad considered this for quite some time, at the end of which he said, 'Yes, I take your point.'

When it came to French though, that was a different ball game altogether. Every week, two of the fifth form had to join Mrs Dunsmuir at her top table for lunch and the conversation had to be conducted in French, of which Mrs Dunsmuir knew not a word. Mr Conrad was only too happy to join us in a discussion about her character, and I seem to remember that among many derogatory phrases the word 'vache' could be heard at regular intervals! At the end of lunch, Mrs Dunsmuir would say 'I do think the girls' French is improving, don't you Mr Conrad?'

'I don't think you know just how much,' he would reply.

He really was a bit of a rogue, generally smelling of beer and tobacco. He was a very tall man, with a long thin face, and looked positively gaunt, truly an angular Anglican, but my friend Fiona and I were very fond of him, and always enjoyed the conspiracy of the lunch table. I suppose we were 'teacher's pets'. It now seems absurd to realise just how naive we were.

Our classroom was in what was called Paraffin Castle. It was a small turret across the courtyard from the castle itself, and in the winter it was freezingly cold, being heated by one paraffin heater, which gave off much more smell than it did heat. After three French lessons, and in my case, every maths class, I asked Fiona, 'When Mr Conrad leans over you to see your work, does he put his hands right inside your gym tunic?'

'Yes,' she said, 'but I don't know why.'

'He does the same to me.' I gave the matter great consideration, and then decided, 'Poor Mr Conrad – his hands must be cold!'

My greatest joy at St Marie's was the elocution and drama classes, taken by Miss Lawrie, who came to us once a week from the Edinburgh College of Speech and Drama. It was always the highlight of my week.

When I left St. Marie's, having achieved a very generous 13% for maths (fortunately the other subjects fared rather better); it was time to decide which drama school I should go to.

The Glasgow one had just opened, but I really didn't want to go back to Newton Mearns. To be honest I found it stultifying. It seemed to me that there you joined Whitecraigs Tennis Club, married the boy next door, one Daddy would buy the house, and the other Daddy furnished it, and there you would sit and set, like a blancmange.

The decision had to be the Edinburgh College of Speech and Drama, and it was so right. Edinburgh is the most marvellous town in which to be a student, and it also meant that I could continue my exams for the London Academy of Music and Dramatic Art. I was now ready to take my Silver and Gold medal exams and then the ALAM exam, but I had to get them with Honours or I would have felt that I had failed!

It also meant that I was reunited with Miss Lawrie, but most importantly for me, and definitely the icing on the cake, was being taught by Miss Ida Watt. She was, and is, the most inspirational person I think I've ever met, and she is a very dear friend.

I stayed in a YWCA hostel for business women in Inverleith Terrace, which was only a tram ride away from College, but it was quite a long uphill walk when I ran out of money!

I got to know the telephone operators very well, because I used to phone home twice a week, and always reversed the charges, and they would say, 'Are you broke again, Audrey?'

During my first year I went home most weekends, but I couldn't believe my ears when one Saturday my father said, 'Would you like to audition for the next Giffnock Theatre play – it's a comedy, and the part is that of a 17-year-old drama student?'

Needless to say this 17-year-old drama student jumped at the chance, read for the casting committee, and got the part. Mind you, drama students were fairly thin on the ground in Newton Mearns in those days so I don't think there was much competition. Nonetheless I was just so grateful to think of all those Sunday rehearsals which I knew I would enjoy immensely, and then the joy of playing to a real audience. The Chairman, Tom Craston, said, 'I'm glad you're going to join us, Audrey, because now we have a professional producer. I think you've met him, it's Rikki Fulton!'

I tried, after a few moments, to return my jaw to a semi-normal position, it had dropped so much. 'Thank you, Tom,' I squeaked. 'I'll really look forward to it.' I calmed down quickly, and tried to breathe. I was going to see him every Sunday, and be directed by him. I thought I'd died and gone to heaven. My Wishing Tree had done it again!

The next few weeks were utter bliss, and much as I loved college, I couldn't wait for Sundays. The more I got to know him, the more head over heels I fell in love with him. He was so handsome, with the most wonderful voice, and his kindness and understanding shone through his direction. But above all there was his sense of humour, which was unsurpassable.

How I envied his wife, Ethel! Whenever Rikki mentioned my

name she dismissed me as 'that gushing little schoolgirl'. Sadly, I think truth was on her side!

We were halfway through rehearsals for the play, which had the strange title *Little Lambs Eat Ivy*, when Rikki called us all together and announced that he was handing the production over to Jimmy Sutherland, as he, himself, was going to London the following day. He had got his first big break in show business, and was going to compère the Joe Loss Show for BBC Radio.

I felt numb, but managed to mumble the usual 'Congratulations and Good Luck' platitudes before running from the room, knowing I was in great danger of making a complete idiot of myself. As we drove home my father looked at me anxiously, and asked if I was feeling all right.

'Yes,' I lied.

When we turned into our driveway I said I wanted some fresh air and ran off into the wood to my Wishing Tree. I wished I had an axe so that I could destroy it but, when I got there, it was looking so beautiful that I just climbed on to my branch, and cried my eyes out. I vowed that never again would I fall in love. That way, I could never be hurt.

I cried off and on for days, and was thoroughly miserable. It can't have been much fun for anyone around, but my mother, who was wonderful, thought she knew a schoolgirl 'crush' when she saw one, and was endlessly sympathetic. But even she couldn't guess just how deep my misery was.

College was an enormous help, especially if I was in one of Miss Watt's productions. That really focused my concentration, and my college friends understood exactly what I was feeling. After all, no one knows more about a broken heart than a teenage drama student!

My only consolation was writing to Rikki every week, but the extraordinary thing is, he always replied.

After the Joe Loss Show, he went on to even greater heights when he took over the Showband Show in April 1953. This was the Cyril Stapleton Orchestra, with celebrity guests. Rikki wrote the script with Lew Schwarz, and then was the chat-show host.

He fell hook, line and sinker for Rosemary Clooney, who apparently was absolutely adorable, even though, at the time, she was having a lot of problems with her husband José Ferrer. But the most memorable star they had on the programme had to be Frank Sinatra. Rikki, like millions of other people, thought he was the greatest singer in the world, and he couldn't believe he was going to be standing at the microphone with him. What would he be like? Would he behave like the big star he was? Would he be temperamental, would he be impossible to work with?

He turned out to be a delight.

Rikki asked him if he was happy with the script he had been given. Frank assured him that he was, and Rikki said that he tended to ad lib (that has to be the understatement of the century). 'Don't worry, Rik,' said Frank, 'you just do your own thing and I'll follow you.' And he did!

Rikki treasured the recording of that programme above all else, but I must say the 'transatlantic accent' he was using, which was so fashionable in the fifties, rather grates on the ear nowadays. I'm just so glad he grew out of it!

Nonetheless, accent or not, it changed the shape of my weekends.

The Showband Show was on at one o'clock on a Saturday which meant I never went home until the afternoon, because if there was any hold-up with the train I might not have got home in time to hear it, and that was just unthinkable. So, I never left Edinburgh until the last notes of the signature tune had faded into the distance.

Something else that was fading into the distance was our correspondence. I was allowing college life and the social student life to take over, and I was at last accepting that my dream of being with Rikki was just that – a dream.

In my last term at college I got my ALAM with Honours, and the next and last exam would be the LRAM. Fate however intervened in the form of an audition for the Byre Theatre.

I couldn't believe it when I was offered a season there. Now I had to decide between going to London to take my LRAM or going to the Byre. And you won't be surprised to learn that within days I was setting off for St Andrews.

2

LEARNING TO WORK IN A BYRE

If you go to the Byre Theatre today you will find a thriving successful business with the most up-to-date technology, but the Byre I'm talking about in 1956 was just that – a cowshed!

I think I'm right in saying that it held about 75 of an audience. But when we had a real smash hit on our hands that could be increased to 80 by putting extra seats in the one and only aisle, strictly against fire regulations, but as the Chief of the local Fire Brigade himself always sat there, everyone seemed quite relaxed about it.

The stage was two feet high and two feet from the front row of seats, and the university students got a kick, literally, from stretching their legs out and tripping up the actors. This resulted in a notice being put up saying, 'Please keep your feet off the stage.' Quite a unique prohibition!

We were all paid the same salary – four pounds ten shillings. Out of this we had to pay for our 'digs', meals out, and supply our own clothes for modern productions, and somehow or other we did!

The Byre Theatre was the love child of a dear man, Alec Paterson, who was a writer and journalist for the local paper. He was the one who wrote the crits for the paper, and I don't remember that we ever got a bad review! Alec was financing the season himself, so naturally there wasn't a lot of money about, and apart from the girl in the box office at night, no one was employed except us. The work was very fairly divided – the girls cleaned the dressing rooms and swept out the auditorium, while the boys emptied the bins and struggled with the temperamental and cantankerous old boiler. We relied on it for heating and hot water.

We also needed it in the summer to supplement our salaries. There wasn't room for a bar, so the theatre had no liquor licence, but soft drinks were to be had in the foyer. In those days all soft drinks came in glass bottles, which, when returned, gave us the money we so badly needed. It was now the turn of the boys to stoke the boiler to bursting point, so that by the interval the audience would be so parched with thirst they would drink countless bottles of lemonade, and, as in the days of three-act plays, there were two intervals. It was, as they say, 'a nice little earner'.

I can't think of a happier way to enter the profession than by way of the Byre. Una MacLean was the leading lady, and her husband Roy Boucher was the director, and because, perhaps, they set the tone, I can't remember any rows or unpleasantness throughout the entire season, and that's pretty unusual! There were also two other girls from the Edinburgh Drama College. Nora MacElvie – who had the most wonderful sense of humour – and Evelyn Elliot, who went on to be described, rightly, as 'the lovely Evelyn Elliot' when she became a presenter for the BBC. Which reminds me of an episode of which I am truly ashamed.

There was a very upmarket dress shop, Greensmith Downes, which we passed every day when we went for lunch, and one day, as the boys went on ahead, we girls stood open-mouthed at the dress in the window. It was one to die for – the most beautiful shade of dark-green velvet with small clusters of pale pink ostrich feathers around the scooped neckline. The top was very fitted and then flared out in a full skirt with more feathers around the hem. For a whole week we drooled over it, at least the rest of us did, but Evelyn was spared that because her parents used to come up every weekend and took her to lunch on Saturday to a restaurant none of us could possibly afford.

That night, after the performance, we were larking about in the dressing room as usual, when Evelyn walked in wearing 'the dress'. She looked absolutely stunning. It fitted her slim figure perfectly, and her fair hair against the green velvet was really beautiful. We stared at her in absolute silence, which was eventually broken by Una saying, 'You'll never guess what I bought today,' and she pulled off her skirt to reveal a pair of navy-blue gym knickers.

We gathered round her saying, 'I don't think I've ever seen such fantastic knickers, do you think they might still have some,' and 'Were they horribly expensive, they certainly look as though they would be.'

When we turned round we found that Evelyn had silently left the room. The dress was never mentioned again.

Working on such a tiny stage presented a number of problems. First of all there wasn't room for a stage set, so all the scenery had to be painted on the walls. Then there was a difficulty with the acoustics. Naturally there was no need for microphones, but if the people in the adjoining house had their radio turned fully up it sounded louder than we did, so someone would phone them, and ask, very politely, if they would be kind enough to turn it down, and they always did.

I think, though, the worst thing of all had to be our exits and entrances. The exit Down Right wasn't at all difficult, but the exit Down Left was a nightmare. Down Right took you into a tiny area at the door into the courtyard, whereas Down Left you were immediately faced with a steel ladder set into the wall. This you had to climb, and you would find yourself in the two dressing rooms, one for the boys and the other for the girls. That was bad enough if it was a modern play, but if it was a costume piece! All

I can say, from experience, is that climbing a vertical ladder in a crinoline takes some doing.

When I think of the ambitious productions we put on I can't believe how we did it. One of these was Shakespeare's *The Taming of the Shrew*, and being such a small company of course we had to double most of the parts. Una was playing the leading part of Katherine and I played her sister Bianca, and also a servant boy. This entailed the dreaded Exit Left as Bianca, Enter Right as the servant boy – all in the space of four minutes. I would make a dignified exit stage left, clamber up the ladder and run to my dressing room, tearing off my 'Bianca' clothes as I ran. Now down to my underwear, I hauled on the servant boy's tunic, and changed my hairstyle. Then it was along the corridor, down the fire escape, across the courtyard, and I finally arrived to Enter Right, hopefully looking cool, calm and collected.

This was all very well in good weather, but if it rained or snowed I was in real trouble. I would exit left with curly hair, and having come down the fire escape and crossed the courtyard, in pouring rain, would reappear stage right with dead straight hair dripping everywhere!

Nothing like that seemed to bother us then. We were all young, we were doing what we enjoyed most, and however small the amount, we were being paid for it.

One of the actors in the company was Tom Watson, and I was delighted to see him again, because I had met him many times at the Giffnock Players. So, when I arrived rather nervously for my first professional work, it was a joy to find someone I knew. I think he guessed that I was somewhat lacking in confidence to start with because he was so very kind to me. We got on famously and spent quite a lot of time together. What more could anyone ask? I was in beautiful St Andrews, which was and is one of my favourite places. I spent all my childhood holidays there with my grandmother. Her father had been very well known in the town, and we were told that on the day of his funeral every shop in the town closed, and he was buried in the Cathedral cemetery. All of which made me feel as though I really belonged there.

The Byre Theatre season ended in January, and I was to get my first experience of 'resting', in other words, being out of work. My sister Doreen had had a very short time out of work but nothing on God's earth could have persuaded her to stand in a dole queue in the short time before she became a demonstrator with the Electricity Board. Or perhaps I just needed the money more than she did. I reckoned that my parents had spent an enormous amount of money on my education, far more than they ever had to spend on Doreen, so from now on I was going to stand on my own two feet.

The nearest Social Security office was in Turriff Street, and let's just say it wasn't exactly surrounded by listed buildings. When I told my mother that I was going there that afternoon, she thought I was joking, but when she realised that I was serious, she insisted on coming with me. I didn't think that was a good idea but she would not be dissuaded and, when she said she was ready and I saw what she was wearing, my heart sank. A mink coat, and diamonds, for Turriff Street!

I was lucky enough to be interviewed by a very kind man who took down all the necessary details about the work I had just done, when I had become unemployed and when I could reasonably expect to be employed again. At that point my mother took over. With her best Newton Mearns accent, she informed the clerk, 'My daughter is an actress, but if you have nothing suitable for her in the theatre, she would consider taking employment as a mannequin.'

The clerk and I looked at each other and both swallowed hard. With an enviably straight face the clerk said, 'I think it only fair to tell you, Mrs Craig-Brown, that we don't often have requests from either the theatre or the fashion world in Turriff Street, but, should one occur, I can assure you Audrey will be top of the list.'

My mother patted his hand reassuringly, said, 'I'm sure you'll do your best,' and with that she swept out.

'It looks as though I shall be signing on for quite some time,' I said to him.

'I wouldn't be so sure,' he replied. 'I have a feeling you'll probably find something for yourself.'

'I shall certainly try,' I said, and followed in the direction my mother had taken, thinking that my big sister has a lot more wisdom than I have!

When I caught up with her, I said, 'Mummy, what was all that about being a mannequin?'

'But you are, you were trained for it.'

'Was I? I wish someone had told me.'

'Audrey, don't be absurd, don't you remember modelling all those lovely frocks for Mr Lindsay?'

'For goodness sake, Mummy, I was nine years old!'

'Age has nothing to do with it – you are a trained mannequin,' she said in a voice that brooked no argument.

I had quite forgotten about that episode in my life.

In those days there was a very upmarket brand of children's clothes with the label 'Lindsay Maid' and one of Mummy's bridge friends was Ada Paterson, who was their dress designer. One afternoon she asked Mummy if she would allow me to model for Mr Lindsay. Apparently he was making a whole wardrobe of clothes for the Duke of Norfolk's daughter and I was exactly the same size, so every now and then, Mummy and I would go to Mr Lindsay's showroom and I would wear all these exquisite frocks. Of course they weren't going to pay a nine-year-old, but at the end of our session Mr Lindsay would say, 'Audrey, you can have anything you choose from my showroom to take home.'

Well, talk about an Aladdin's cave! There were summer dresses with beautiful hand smocking, and then the party dresses in velvets, taffetas and lace. That was always the rail my mother headed for, but to no avail. Every time, I chose the same thing – a pair of shorts!

Still, my mother had given me an idea. I hadn't lived at home since I left Hutchie, and I certainly didn't want to sit around doing nothing, so I used some of my dole money to take modelling classes from a lady called Margo Bannister. She was the leader of the fashion scene in Glasgow and was, deservedly, very popular – as was her husband Fred – on the social scene. He was the manager of the well-known Marlborough function suites, and the Bannisters were greatly sought-after because everyone knew that if Fred and Margo were at your party it was bound to be a success.

When I finished my last class with Margo she made a phone call, and the following day I started work at Pettigrew and Stephens as their in-house Junior Miss model!

This involved modelling the clothes in the restaurant, and chatting to the customers. I enjoyed it very much, but I think that was because I knew I was just filling in time until my next theatre work came along. As it turned out that was much quicker than I had expected.

In March I heard that Harry Douglas was holding auditions in the George Hotel for a summer season in Aberdeen. I went along, and was lucky enough to be cast as the juvenile for the company. I remember walking on air all the way back to Pettigrews, and then floating among the tables for the rest of the day.

We began rehearsals in May, so my modelling career was fairly short-lived, but I could now say that I was a trained model, and who knows, it might just come in handy in the future.

The first day of rehearsal is always a bit nerve-wracking, when you meet the people with whom you are going to spend morning, noon, and night, for the entire summer. It turned out to be a very pleasant company, and there I made two lifelong friends. The first was the marvellous Walter Carr, the kindest and most gentle man, with a brilliant talent for comedy. And his homemade three-fruit marmalade was out of this world!

The second was John Gayford. He was the male juvenile of the company, so naturally we played opposite each other nearly all the time. We got on wonderfully well together and it really was like a brother and sister relationship. Sadly though, the season was a bit of a disaster, and poor Harry must have lost a lot of money. We guessed there must be financial problems when the stage manager came round the dressing rooms five minutes after the curtain came down, and removed all the light bulbs around our make-up mirrors!

Poor Harry never stood a chance. We were in the Beach Pavilion which was right on the sea front, and some distance from the town centre. It was a barn of a place, and Aberdeen can be quite windy, so if it was gusty in the town, it would be blowing a gale on the beach. The really big problem though was the fact that the beautiful His Majesty's Theatre had the Whatmore Players, an excellent and very popular company who had been coming to Aberdeen for decades.

There really was no contest, so it wasn't long before we read on the noticeboard that we were to close in a fortnight, some time before the season was due to end. We were all very sad about it, and especially for Harry, who had put so much time, effort and money into the project.

I had resigned myself to going back to Pettigrews and the rest of the company were phoning their agents asking them to get work as soon as possible. I don't know where Leonard Fenton went, but he ended up playing the doctor in *Eastenders*, and Mary Marquis went on to become, arguably, the best presenter BBC Scotland has ever had.

During our last week, unknown to us, David Stuart came to see a performance. He, with Marjorie Dence, ran Perth Rep, which had a tremendously good reputation. He came round to my dressing room after the curtain call and when he left I just sat there in a stunned silence for quite a few minutes, then I rushed into the corridor just as John ran out of his room. We both started jabbering at the same time, 'You'll never guess!' We both stopped. John said, 'David Stuart?'

I nodded, 'And you?'

'He's invited me to Perth too,' he said.

We hugged each other for a very long time. Life was good, very good.

3

PERTH AND BEYOND

Perth Rep was a large company, because one half of the company would be touring while the other half played in Perth. It was an excellent arrangement because it gave us much more time for rehearsing, and although there were a lot of us, it still felt like being part of a family.

David and Marjorie had worked in theatre together and they had both seen the beautiful Perth Theatre. It was, and is, a gem of a Victorian theatre, and Marjorie Dence's father bought it for her. David and Marjorie were never an 'item' as we know it nowadays but they had a very happy professional relationship. David, however, was an actor, and therefore one of us. He was the kindest of men, but was never really able to feel he *was* one of us. Perhaps being the Artistic Director weighed heavily on him. Mind you, I don't imagine his mother helped!

She was a tiny little grey-haired lady and everyone loved her. She was always known as Mama Stuart, and she, like David, was very artistic and musical, and also absent-minded. I remember in one play David had to play the violin, an instrument with which he was not familiar, but Mama was, so it was arranged that Mama would play the violin in the wings while David mimed onstage. All went well for many nights until Mama was caught up in a conversation in the circle bar and missed the end of interval call. This, of course, was long before there were mobile phones and pagers, so an assistant stage manager had to run all the way up to the circle to tell Mama she was late. By this time the curtain was up, and David was poised with his violin and bow, for a long, long, time. The silence was at last broken by a voice from the circle, *loudly,* 'Don't worry darling, Mummy's coming,' followed by a clattering of feet from the circle, then from the stalls, then into the wings, then a loud stage whisper, 'Ready when you are, David, darling.'

John and I were cast as the juveniles in our first play at Perth. It was Agatha Christie's *Murder at the Vicarage,* and it was a joy to be working together so soon. We had become so used to acting together that we both knew exactly how the other worked. When it came to learning lines, I was lucky to be what is known as a quick study, but John sometimes found lines a bit of a chore. So, unknown to him, I used to learn his lines as well as my own in our scenes, just in case he ever forgot his – which, of course, he never did. The strange thing about that is that today John can quote lines from plays that we've done, and I couldn't even tell you the title!

Perth is such a special place to work in that it attracted a number of stalwarts who would stay for not just a year or two, but for decades. There were two leading ladies, Jane Cain the blonde, whose husband Eddy Bailey was a producer, and Valerie Lush the brunette, whose husband Wilfred Bentley was also a producer, known to the company as Bill. They both had beautiful homes, and were employed all the year round, because although the Rep closed in the summer and a Variety show took over, the Company went out on tour, two tours in fact, one to the Highlands and the other to the Lowlands.

Jane was famous as the voice of the Speaking Clock on the telephone, and when Val left Perth eventually, she did a lot of television, perhaps best known as the French housekeeper in Peter Mayle's *A Year in Provence.*

One of the leading men was the wonderful Leon Sinden. What

a joy he was to work with. He liked Perth so much that he bought a house there, where he still lives. He would probably be best known to television audiences as the lawyer in *Take the High Road*.

The summer tours were much sought after because they were so totally different from working in a civilised theatre, especially a beautiful Victorian one!

The first one I went on was out of this world, but my goodness it was hard work. Being a junior member of the company meant that I had to do stage management work as well as my acting roles. This involved helping to take down the sets after each performance, and loading up the lorry with scenery, props, costumes, and company luggage. Then after a very few hours' sleep, it would be on to the next venue, where we would unload all the scenery, props, costumes and company luggage, and prepare for the evening's performance!

Sometimes we would be very lucky and spend four or five nights in the same place. This felt like being on holiday, because although we still had to change the set every day at least we didn't have to drive around so much.

We thought Stornaway would be marvellous because we were to be there for nearly a week, and we all looked forward to it, to having a bit of a rest, but most of all to meeting the people who lived there.

Our arrival did not bode well. As we approached the harbour, one of our actresses accosted a crew member and asked him, 'Where does one disembark?'

'I don't know,' was the reply, 'but you get off here.'

We gathered at the top of the gangway and smiled happily at the group of elderly men below. They stared back at us with barely-disguised contempt and as we came down the gangway they said loudly, 'These will be the play actors.' Trying hard not to seem like the lepers they made us feel, we marched confidently to our hotel.

What a difference we found there! The owner and his staff could not have been more welcoming, our rooms were clean and comfortable, and they were even prepared to give us a meal when we came back after the evening's performance. Nonetheless, we approached our first play *Tobias and the Angel* with some trepidation, but in fact we need not have worried. Mr Bridie's play was happily received by an enthusiastic audience.

We went back to our hotel for a most welcome supper, and mentioned to the manager that the people of Stornoway seemed to keep quite late hours, as the main street seemed very busy for that time of night.

'Oh, that's not the locals – those are the Norwegian sailors. Their navy has been anchored here for a week and they sail tomorrow. They are a nice crowd, just a wee bit wild at times, and we're fairly going to miss them in the bar!'

After our meal, as usual, we sat around talking, something actors always do at the end of a performance.

When you come offstage you really have to unwind.

I know that some people think that actors are shallow and superficial, but nothing could be further from the truth. When you work with people for the run of a play or a tour, you get to know them very well indeed, and it might be ten years before you meet again. But when you do, it's as though a decade hasn't existed.

Back to Stornoway. Having 'tired the sun with talking, and sent him down the sky', we all went to our rooms for a well-earned rest.

My room was on the third floor, and I was never so glad to get into bed, but as always I had to read my book, a habit I got into from a very early age and have never lost.

I was engrossed in a biography of Oscar Wilde when I felt a chill wind in the room. I looked up, to see a drunken Norwegian sailor who had pushed up the window and was now climbing into my bedroom.

Using all the technique I had learned at drama school, I screamed the place down, and then pushed him over the window sill. When the Cavalry arrived, in the form of the men of Perth Rep, they found me in a state of shock, firmly convinced that I would be convicted of murder, or if I was very lucky, perhaps getting away with manslaughter. I had thrown a man to his death from my third-floor window. I steeled myself to look at the lane below but there was no sign of a corpse. In fact, there was no sign of anything.

It was at this point that one of my rescuers pointed out that although my room was on the third floor the hotel was built on a hill and I was actually on ground level!

I can only presume that my Norwegian sailed home the next day with a massive hangover, and bruises for which he couldn't begin to account.

The tours really were not to be missed, although they did have some bleak moments, like our digs in Fort William where our landlady belonged to the Wee Free Church. We thought she was joking on the Sunday when she took the budgie's swing out of his cage and then covered the cage with a cloth so that not a cheep was heard. But we realised she meant it when she threw us out in the afternoon because she caught us playing cards on the Sabbath! Our one and only day of relaxation had to be spent trekking around trying to find accommodation. Fortunately we eventually found a boarding house whose owners didn't have quite such religious fervour!

Going back to Perth was even more exciting this time because I was now renting my own flat. The first season I had had a bedsitter, and shared a kitchen with the wonderful Edith Macarthur. I was totally in awe of her (still am if the truth be told!), and this was the first time I had had to cook for myself and it couldn't have been more basic – whereas Edie was adding herbs to things, and even putting sherry in her soup! I had never known such sophistication.

What was really wonderful this time was that my best friend from college, Hilary, was joining the company, so naturally we shared the flat. It had a rather odd layout. It was the very top flat of a beautiful terraced house which looked onto the North Inch in Perth. It had obviously been the nursery flat and had a large living room, two bedrooms, kitchen and bathroom, but what was odd about it was that the bath was in the kitchen! And I remember that only too well.

One day Hilary went out to lunch with her parents who had come up from Edinburgh. They were the most lovely people, full of life and vitality, and their kindness and hospitality when I was at college are something I will never forget. Anyway, Hilary was wearing a beautiful Hebe suit which they had given her for her birthday and when we went home after the evening's play she was still wearing it.

We both shared the chores in our flat, and I was using all my culinary expertise to make scrambled eggs on toast. I was beating the eggs in a bowl while Hilary set the table, after which she came and sat on the edge of the bath and I started to tell her about a cartoon I had seen in the *Sunday Post*. It was a pair of Glasgow women on a bus, sitting opposite a mother and her small son who had his head firmly jammed in a saucepan. One woman is saying to the other, 'Imagine taking a wean out in a filthy saucepan like that!' To illustrate the point, I turned our saucepan over Hilary's head, not knowing that she had poured the eggs into it. She sat there speechless, on the bath, with eggs dripping down her hair, and all over her beautiful green Hebe suit. I can't think why we are the best of friends to this day, but we are. She must have a very forgiving nature!

Our landlord was an elderly man called Mr Dawes, who lived on the ground floor. He was very pleasant, but we were very aware that he kept a stern eye on our going out and coming in. He could be very easily shocked so we were grateful that he was hard of hearing. One Sunday evening we had a party, and as Mr

Dawes lived on the ground floor he couldn't hear any of the noise we were making. No, the problem occurred the next morning. Hilary's boyfriend Brian had stayed the night but he had to get back to Edinburgh by lunchtime for his law exams. Hilary and I had to go to rehearsal, so we wished him luck and left.

Mr Dawes usually went out about ten and Brian intended to leave unseen whenever he heard the door shut.

Only it didn't. The only sound that could be heard was the clattering of paint pots. Mr Dawes had decided that particular Monday was just the day for a bit of DIY. He was going to paint all the treads on the staircase white, starting of course from the top flat. Brian now had to risk ruining our reputation, and his own, remembering that his father was a highly respected public figure, and facing the shocked horror of Mr Dawes as he left a footprint on every tread of the newly painted staircase. Cowardice prevailed. He stayed put, missed his exam, and didn't manage to escape until it was dark and he heard Mr Dawes busy in his kitchen preparing his supper. He told us about it in an irate phone call, and that was the last we heard from him. I often wonder if he did become a lawyer. I do hope so.

One thing we always looked forward to in the season was the arrival of the 'Comedy Team'. This consisted of Roddy MacMillan, Clem Ashby and Roy Kinnear.

They would be 'imported' for Scots comedies, like *Bachelors Are Bold*. We adored the practical jokes they played on each other, and us, and the audiences loved them.

Roy enjoyed Perth Theatre so much that he stayed on to the end of the season, and the next.

We had a most odd relationship. We had met often at Hilary's home when I was in Edinburgh, and we had enjoyed our meetings, seeming to share the same sense of humour.

When Roy came to Perth for a prolonged stay, I suppose that it was only natural that we would spend a lot of time with each other, which we did. We never lived together, but we so enjoyed each other's company.

As well as playing in Perth we also went further afield to Forfar, Brechin and Kirkcaldy, and my abiding memory of the Kirkcaldy private bus run is peeling oranges for Roy. He had some sort of allergy to citrus fruits and couldn't touch them, so I would peel them and feed them to him while he kept his hands safely in a brown paper bag. On our return to Perth, when the bus dropped us off at the theatre, we would cross the road to the café, where we always had the same supper, baked beans and chips. Nutritious and cheap!

At that time Roy was very much in love with a girl in London, and between them they had worked out a way of keeping in touch.

Our modest supper always had to end by 11.45pm, because by 11.50pm Roy had to be in the public phone box to talk to Jan. She would also be in a public phone box in London, and would phone Roy at the Perth number, and *reverse* the charges. Roy of course would accept them, and they could talk for ages.

Then Roy and I would stroll through Perth to our respective flats discussing the evening's performance, and what Jan had had to say that night.

I will never forget a female member of the company saying, 'What on earth can you find attractive in Roy Kinnear?' I could only tell her that I thought he was one of the most sincere men I had ever met, he was the soul of kindness, and most of all he made me laugh.

At the end of the day he didn't marry Jan, but had a most happy marriage with the actress Carmel Cryan, until his untimely death during the filming of a remake of *The Three Musketeers* when he fell from his horse as they galloped across a bridge. It was a tragic accident, mourned by his many fans and friends, and I count myself among them.

I stayed at Perth for one more season. Hilary had left by then, so I had the flat to myself, which I rather enjoyed. I think I've always been something of a loner, until I met Rikki. Then I was told that someone from the Glasgow Drama College was joining the company and was looking for somewhere to stay. Obviously, my spare bedroom was the answer, but sharing with a stranger can be a bit daunting. However Nan Kerr and I were willing to give it a try.

We did not get off to a good start!

I was in my theatre dressing room when we met, and her first words to me instead of any form of greeting were, as she rather scornfully fingered the pale blue shirt I was wearing, 'Still wearing the old school blouse, I see.' As I said, not an endearing start to a friendship, and to make it worse she was absolutely right!

4

PASSPORT TO PIMLICO

After very happy years at Perth, I felt it was time to brave the unknown, and head for London. I had no agent, no prospects, no money, but thanks to dear John I did have somewhere to stay.

He now had a flat in St George's Drive in Pimlico, where he stayed with his friend, and was kind enough to ask me to join them. This I did with the greatest of pleasure.

Thus began, in 1958, what I suppose could be considered my Bohemian phase!

I was incredibly lucky to go to an open audition for Leatherhead Theatre and spend a season with them and what an interesting time that was. Not only did well-known stars come there, but it was also a learning experience for people like Vanessa Redgrave and Simon Williams.

Vanessa was kind enough to invite me to her 21st birthday party which was lovely, but instead of a lavish showbusiness ball it was a table for about ten, without any pretension or ceremony, just like Vanessa herself.

Back home at St George's Drive our *ménage à trois* was flourishing. John's friend Peter was a sous-chef at the Dorchester Hotel, which meant that our housekeeping bills were minimal. Peter would phone from work to hear what we would like for dinner, and bring it to us. We ate very well and, fortunately, he was never caught. Apparently what the chefs did was to wait

29

until the meat chill room was open, then put a plastic bag over the top of their hair, take out whatever meat or poultry was asked for and hide it under their high chef's hat. They could walk about all day with chicken or steaks on their heads! Every now and then they would be 'frisked' on their way out, and if they were caught with any food they would be instantly dismissed, but somehow or other Peter managed to escape discovery.

We did have a slight problem with John's parents. Although his mother knew he was gay, his father, who was a retired Brigadier, would have been horrified. But in a way he found the solution for us. When I moved in he thought John and I were in a relationship and thoroughly approved. I used to get very saucy birthday and Christmas cards from him, and he even said to his wife, 'Isn't it splendid that John and Audrey have their own chef?'

John's flat was in the basement, and had only two rooms. Naturally the boys had the bedroom, and I had a divan in the sitting room. That was absolutely fine except when we were having a party. Then I had no choice other than to wait till the last guest had left before I could go to bed. We tended to have rather a lot of parties, with Peter doing the catering, and it's amazing how many guests you can cram into a tiny flat when you take off all the doors! Of course all the guests would be John and Peter's friends, except one, he would be my boyfriend of the moment, so there would be 38 of them, and two of us. Invariably I would end up shielding him in a corner, telling the rest of the room, 'Don't even think about it, this one's mine.'

This was a time of auditions for commercials and films, and I suppose for self-assessment. I was cast for a small part in a film, which involved rolling about in a haystack with Bill Travers, but the night before I was due to film I had a phone call to say the scene had been cut, and thus ended my film career. My agent still sent me for interviews for films, but by now I knew it was useless and I also knew the format. This was the day of the Rank Starlets and I certainly didn't qualify. I would dutifully turn up at the film director's office, and as I walked in they often showed a spark of interest, we would chat quite animatedly, until the dreaded moment when he would say, 'Could you turn round and let me see your profile.' And that would be that! Sometimes by flattering candlelight I can look quite reasonable, but in profile I look like Punch, with what is called my 'determined chin' and a nose that instead of turning up and being delightfully retroussé stubbornly turns down towards that chin.

So there was going to be no Rank stardom for me, not that it bothered me at all (though it bothered my agent) because I was enjoying the theatre so much – but even there, I had to accept my limitations. More than anything I loved playing comedy, and at one point during the Leatherhead season when I was playing the tomboy young sister in *Picnic* (a gift of a part) I was told that the top West End agent Peter Crouch had been in, thought I was star material and would be coming back to see the next production. Sadly in the next play I was the uninspired daughter in a very pedestrian play, the title of which I can't even remember, and so it was Goodbye Mr Crouch.

I also had a chastening moment in the theatre I loved so much. We were playing a farce, *Dry Rot*, in which again I had the most wonderful part of Beth the maid. In those days my hair was long and straight, so in a scene when I was supposed to be sleep-walking I combed my hair over my face, and what with that and a Victorian nightdress, it was very difficult for the men to decide which way I was facing. I got some fulsome reviews for that production and these were not well received by the three actors who had joined us for the production.

What they had not realised was that back stage there were only two dressing rooms, one for the women and another for the men. The partition between the two was very flimsy and didn't reach to the roof, so every word that was spoken could be heard in the adjoining room, and what I heard when I was alone in the dressing room is something I will never forget. To put it mildly they were not impressed with the crits, and discussed my acting, and myself, in no uncertain terms. It is quite startling to hear people, with whom you thought you were on good terms, saying what they *really* think about you. The three were Stanley Meadows, who I'm told came into an inheritance and left the theatre, Derek Martinus, who became a theatre director, and Peter Bowles – need I say more? I think he is superb. Has there been a more suave performer since George Sanders? I enjoy his acting every bit as much as he disliked mine!

When the Leatherhead season ended, I was once again out of work, but fortunately in London there was always some sort of employment and I either worked in a coffee bar just round the corner, owned by friends, or in a telephone answering service, where one of their clients was Barbara Cartland's daughter, at that time the Countess of Dartmouth, soon to become Princess Diana's stepmother when she married Earl Spencer. I hope she never found out just how many of her conversations were overheard by the girls in the exchange.

It was about this time that I landed my dear father with a bit of a problem. He was an elder in Broom Church, and the elderly minister was retiring to be replaced by the charming and handsome Neilson Peterkin, who had a wife to match. What a beautiful couple they were. Neilson has since died, but the lovely Elsa, thankfully, is still here.

Of course Neilson wanted to know his elders and their families, and he had really done his homework. He said to my father, 'I believe you have a daughter who is the wife of a Glasgow Academy boy, they live in the West End and now have two sons at the Academy.'

My father was very happy to assure him this was correct, and then came the dreaded question, which sounded like a line straight out of *Cinderella*. 'But don't you have a younger daughter, one you haven't mentioned?' How my father got out of that one I can't imagine; perhaps he just told the truth – 'she's an out-of-work actress living in a basement flat in Pimlico with two homosexuals' – or perhaps he didn't!

While I was at the Leatherhead Theatre I changed my name. We were about to do Arthur Miller's wonderful play *Death of a Salesman*, when I heard the director saying to the manager of the theatre, 'Who's playing the tart? I bet she's got a double-barrelled name.' That did it! I'd never been happy with a hyphen, and now reverted to my maiden middle name of Matheson.

Perhaps the change of name brought me luck, because shortly after that I was invited to go to Whitby for the season. This was actually much more exciting than it sounds because the director of the company was to be the wonderful Joan Knight, a quite extraordinary woman. We first met at Perth Theatre where she was, at that time, stage manager, and this was to be her first attempt at directing. And how successful it was! After some time directing in England, on the deaths of Marjorie Dence and David Stuart she took over Perth Theatre and made a resounding success of it for decades.

I very much doubt if there was one person who worked for Joan who didn't fall in love with her – she was larger than life in every way. I know the word sounds rather old-fashioned but the best way to describe Joan is jolly. She was one of the most compassionate, caring people I have ever met, with a sense of humour second to none, and if Joan was running a company, it was bound to be a happy one.

The other factor that drew me to Whitby was that Roy Kinnear was joining the company, as was Nan Kerr.

John, Peter and I all went to see Nan off at the station. She, not knowing that Peter had already put all my luggage on the train, bade us an almost tearful farewell. Then, when she found her seat, she discovered that I was sitting next to her. 'What on earth are you doing here?' she yelled. I smiled at her calmly and said,

'The same as you, I'm going to Whitby.'

I found digs in a most comfortable guest house and everything seemed to be going splendidly. I was so looking forward to working with Joan, but then she dropped what for me was a bombshell. Roy wasn't going to be with us. Apparently in the last week he had been offered the part of 'Mr Fixit' in a children's serial produced by STV, and as Joan was not the kind of person to stand in the way of anyone's success, she released him from his contract. His career never looked back.

The actor who was to replace him was Graham Roberts. He seemed to be an extremely nice fellow, but I was determined to have nothing to do with him, because I was still so disappointed that Roy wasn't with us – so it was at least six weeks before we became engaged!

It really was a most romantic setting. We were walking back from the theatre after the evening's performance when Graham suggested we should go through the park. It was a beautiful warm night and the perfume of the evening's flowers was glorious. We sat on a park bench and he asked me to marry him.

I did need a few minutes to think about it, but eventually, common sense prevailed. I knew the chance of ever meeting the love of my teenage years was remote. Rikki, as far as I knew, was still happily married to Ethel. I had turned down quite a number of offers of marriage but Graham was different. I liked him tremendously, and still do! He was kind and caring and very popular. Most of my proposals had come from men in the business world, lawyers, actuaries, doctors. Only one of each, I hasten to add! I knew none of those could have worked; one of them actually said that because of his status in the town I would have to give up 'this theatre nonsense, and settle down'. He was given very short shrift!

It so happened that my parents had come to visit me, and were staying in the same guesthouse, otherwise we would never have seen each other. Graham saw me to the door and I went in trying to conceal my excitement. My father was fast asleep, but my mother always stayed awake until I came in, reading her book. I tiptoed into their room and Mummy pointedly put her forefinger on the paragraph she was reading, and when I whispered to her that Graham had asked me to marry him, she gave a long suffering sigh, said, 'Not another one', and went back to her book.

I had always thought that when a daughter told her parents that she wanted to marry it would be one of the most important days of her life, but obviously that didn't apply as far as I was concerned, and I went to bed feeling quite dejected.

The next day however was rather better. Graham did all the right things. He addressed Daddy as 'Sir' and asked if they could meet at the end of the night's play, when he formally asked my father's permission to marry me. This was given, although Daddy had many reservations about it. He was more than happy to be the father of an actress but he hadn't counted on her marrying an actor!

It was the most marvellous summer. It was 1959 and the sun shone every day. We rehearsed each morning, spent the afternoon on the beach and did a play, mostly my favourite, comedy, at night. Graham and I were tremendously happy, especially when we were both invited back to Perth for the season – we thought that would give us time to plan our future.

While we were there Graham was offered work as a producer at the Altrincham Theatre. This was a well-known amateur group with their own beautiful theatre and a professional producer. The standard was extremely high – one of the leading ladies was Paula Tilbrook who now plays Betty in *Emmerdale*. What a sense of humour she has.

Another bonus was that Graham's mother lived in Chester so we were very near her, but of course before we got to Cheshire, we had to have 'The Wedding'. Graham and I were married by Neilson Peterkin in Broom Church. Princess Margaret had married earlier that year, and somehow or other Broom Church now had the piece of carpet on which the Princess and Lord Snowdon took their vows. From then on all the Broom Brides were married on the same carpet. I just hope the habit died out – it was hardly a good omen.

Then came the reception, held in the Marlborough, and what a dreary affair that was! We had forgotten that because we were marrying in July, all our friends in the theatre would be working, so apart from a few relatives, nearly all our guests were my mother's bridge friends. Charming people I'm sure, but let's just say they didn't exactly set the heather on fire. My sister had very kindly lent me her wedding dress which was lovely, but I had to go to a hairdresser in Glasgow who had never done my hair before and I hated what he did with it. It's one thing having a 'bad hair day', but not on your wedding day!

Still, perhaps I shouldn't complain. At least the Marlborough was quite good in those days; I understand it later went very downhill and no longer exists. I'm told that just before it expired altogether they were reduced to employing elderly part-time waitresses, and one guest told me of a wedding reception to which she had been invited where the first course was the inevitable melon. The waitress, on being told that a gentleman at her table couldn't take the fruit, removed the plate, but instead of returning it to the kitchen, she marched up to the top table, and in a very loud voice with the broadest Glasgow accent, asked the assembled company, 'Do any o' youse waant this man's melon?' I think it was at this point the bride's mother had hysterics.

Graham and I had a very happy honeymoon at the Kyles of Bute Hydro, where I had gone with the family for many years. It's a strange thing though, but I'm sure any actor will tell you that when you have been constantly working in the theatre, and suddenly stop, even for a short time, you get decidedly twitchy at five to seven. That is when the stage manager calls 'The Half', and woe betide you if you're not in by then to start putting on your make-up. It really felt quite strange to have whole evenings to ourselves.

In no time, it seemed, we were driving down to Altrincham and a completely new sort of life. One in which Graham would be working, but I wouldn't.

We were renting a top flat in a lovely house in Groby Road. I seemed to be fated to live in nursery attics!

It was owned by a charming Italian family, the Valgimilles. There were four sisters, all unmarried – Miss Ina did all the shopping and cooking, Miss Ida ran the house, Miss Beatrice was the games teacher at a local private school and Miss Maria taught Italian in a college, and also had several books published on learning Italian. Somewhere in the distance there were two brothers but we rarely saw them. They seemed to live on the ground floor, and I remember them mostly as vague shadows and unfailingly courteous whenever we met.

It really was a remarkable household. The moment you crossed the threshold, you could feel the love and contentment they created. You won't be surprised to know that they did a tremendous amount of charity work for the people of Manchester, and their generosity also spread far beyond that. They lived very simply, and when, as sometimes happened, they invited me for lunch, it was wonderful to go into their large, warm kitchen which always had the unforgettable smell of home baking. It was there on a wooden bench at their refectory table that I enjoyed perfectly cooked homemade spaghetti, served with only a great deal of butter and a vast amount of cheese. The cheese melted gently into the hot buttered spaghetti, and I don't know when I've ever enjoyed anything more.

Graham was totally involved with the Altrincham Theatre, which left me with a lot of time on my hands, something I had never experienced before, and didn't like. I managed to pass the time by teaching myself how to cook, and discovered a hidden talent (which I no longer have!) for making cakes. This lasted for all of two weeks, when I decided that though chocolate cakes may be filling they were certainly not fulfilling.

I had heard that Oldham Rep had a new and very exciting director so I went to see him, a most charming man, Carl Paulsen.

He cast me in his next production, *The Aspern Papers* by Henry James. I didn't think I was very good in that, so it was a tremendous relief when he cast me in the following production, as Gwendolyn in *The Importance of Being Earnest*. *Now* I knew what I was doing! I adore Oscar Wilde, and have possibly read every book that has been written about him, and to be given the opportunity of speaking some of the wittiest lines in the English language is a memory I treasure. Over many years in the theatre I have played in a number of his plays, but *The Importance* will always be my favourite.

Carl was an extraordinary man. He was very tall and lean, and yes, come to think of it he *did* have a hungry look! The strange thing about him was that he couldn't bear a happy company. If there wasn't a row going on, and there generally was, he would engineer one, to get us all at loggerheads. Why this should have pleased him I can't imagine, and in spite of the fact that we all knew what he was up to, we loved and admired him.

Up until I met him I had the opportunity to work with some of the top West End directors at Leatherhead and not one of them could begin to compare with him.

When we gathered onstage for 'notes' after a morning's rehearsal we all knew what to expect – nothing was ever right. I think my favourite note from him was after a very dreary play when he said, 'Audrey Matheson played her part with all the charm of an air hostess on a very minor airline.'

Dear Carl, he really was an enigma; the more he tried to make us dislike him the more we loved him! It must have been very frustrating for him.

Sometime after I had left Altrincham I was told that he had died. What a loss to the theatre that was. He can only have been in his forties.

The commuting to Oldham from Altrincham was not easy. Graham would drive me into Manchester to the bus station, from where I would take the bus to Oldham, and make my own way back home.

I did have one rather scary moment on my way back home one night after the theatre. I had to go across Manchester to catch the bus back to Altrincham. I had a feeling that I was being followed, so I started to go up side streets, but always where there were people about, and sure enough, the footsteps were just behind me. I decided I'd had enough of this cat and mouse game, and made a run for the main thoroughfare, but he was too quick for me, he grabbed me by the arm and turned me towards him. I'm not quite sure what I expected, possibly a drunk or a drug addict but certainly not the extremely respectable and well-dressed man who held my arm so firmly in his grasp and said, 'Where did you get that skirt?' What kind of perversion is this, I wondered, but I said, 'that is none of your business, but if you really want to know it was made for me.'

At this he became quite belligerent and shook me. I said, 'If you dare to do that again, I shall scream for a policeman.' With that he let me go, but looked so miserable that I had to ask him, 'What is the reason for all this – why are you so angry?'

He began to calm down and explained that he was a fabric designer, and I was wearing one of his designs. His problem was that he designed curtain material, and when he saw me wearing it as a skirt he naturally assumed that someone in the 'Rag Trade' had stolen his design. I was very glad that I was able to reassure him that my skirt was a one-off. My mother had spotted the material, which was a lovely pattern of horses heads on a pale camel background, and knowing how crazy I was about horses, she took it to her dressmaker and asked her to make it into a skirt.

He was mightily relieved, and very apologetic. It would be nice to think that he started to design fashion clothes and made a fortune, but as we never exchanged names, I'll never know.

Graham and I both enjoyed being in Altrincham. He was happy with his theatre, and I loved working for Carl, but all that was to change. Grampian Television in Aberdeen asked Graham to join them as an announcer and he jumped at the chance. We bought a new house in Beechgrove Crescent and hadn't the faintest idea what to do with it! Eventually we got it furnished and settled in (at least Graham did) but as usual apart from a spell with the Whatmore Players there was no work going for me in Aberdeen.

For some time Graham and I had realised that our relationship had changed. Instead of a marriage, we had a loving and abiding friendship. When I realised I could never find enough theatre work in Aberdeen, I asked Graham if we could sit down and discuss it. I told him that I felt I had to go back to London, and that I couldn't promise that I would always be on my own, and that if he wanted to divorce me he had every right to do so. The great problem was that we were so fond of each other, and by the end of our talk we had decided that we would not divorce until one or other of us wanted to remarry.

When I arrived in London in 1963 I rented a small flat in Finchley Road, and yes, it was in the attic! I was sure that one day I would be sharing one with the portrait of Dorian Grey. The very first thing I had to do was to find an agent, and a friend suggested Vincent Shaw. I went to his office and was quite taken aback. He wasn't at all like any other agent I'd met. He looked like a Viking. He was six feet four inches tall, with fair hair and a beard to match. If you remember the lovely singers Nina and Frederick he was the double of Frederick.

He said he would try to get me work and would get in touch.

In the meantime, Giles Havergill was starting up his first season at Watford. What a genius that man is! Who else could

have made the Citizen's Theatre in Glasgow a worldwide name?
I had first met him at Oldham, where he had come as a trainee
from Granada Television, and it was obvious he was going to be
a success. His first production at Watford was *Blithe Spirit*, and
he asked me to play Elvira. I was over the moon – not only was
I working again but it was in a Noel Coward play.

The day after Giles and I had signed the contract, I had a
phone call from Vincent, who said that casting was going on at
Watford and he had put my name forward to play Elvira. I
explained that I already had the part but I was very grateful that
he had put my name forward, and the least I could do was to
pay him half the commission he would have earned had he got
me the part. Then one night he suddenly appeared in my dressing
room and said that after seeing the play he was sure he could
keep me in work. I couldn't have been more delighted. I was
living in London again and the future seemed bright. Just how
bright, I was about to find out.

Vincent hadn't brought his car to Watford, so I was more than
happy to drive him to his flat in Shaftesbury Avenue. I had an
MG sports car at that time which he very much admired. On the
journey back to London we were both aware that we had a
serious sexual attraction to each other. When we arrived at his
flat he invited me in, but I said no. There was so much going on
in my head that I really had to sort out.

Vincent took me out for supper after the play a couple of times
and then announced that the next time he was going to show off
his home cooking and make me a meal at his flat. We both knew
perfectly well what that would lead to and, when I arrived, I was
shown into soft lights, romantic music and the champagne was
on ice. He had even made out a menu for the meal, each item of
which was supposed to be an aphrodisiac! He really shouldn't
have gone to so much trouble – we both knew we were going to
spend the night together.

Even before I met him I had heard of Vincent's love for the

ladies, and their love for him.

After that night I fully understood why. If sexual prowess was included in the Olympics, he would have won every gold medal. He knew exactly how to give a woman a sexual satisfaction which was out of this world and he certainly enjoyed himself along the way! Our affair soon became well known, but I didn't want to move into Shaftesbury Avenue until I had left the Watford Theatre.

Meantime, Giles was about to stage a most ambitious production of *Macbeth*. It was to be very realistic, so the stage was covered in about a foot of earth. This worked well at the dress rehearsal, but from then on we were ploughing our way through mud. The costumes were rather strange as they were all made out of PVC. I was playing Lady Macduff, and my costume was a white PVC full-length tunic slashed at the sides to the waist with thigh-length boots. The boots were certainly useful in the mud, but I did feel that I looked more like a petrol pump attendant than her ladyship!

During the first week of the production a notice went up on the board, saying that the entire company was invited to a supper, on stage, the following evening, and would the ladies please wear long dresses. We dutifully turned up the next night in evening dress, and Giles apologised for all the secrecy but explained that he was to be the host to Princess Margaret and Lord Snowdon. They would see the play and then we would all have supper together. After the performance we went to our dressing rooms to change, and I kept wondering how they were going to clear the stage of all that 'glaur'. The simple answer was, they didn't!

The stage was like something out of *Alice in Wonderland*. Set in the thick mud were tiny, delicate gilt tables, set with sparkling white table cloths, silver cutlery and crystal glasses. I must say making a curtsey in mud is not to be recommended! The meal was lovely, and had apparently been chosen by the Princess. We started with a savoury egg custard smothered in caviar, followed by salmon, which I would guess came from Royal Deeside, and ended with cherries flamed in brandy. Just the thing for a late-night snack!

The small tables were placed very close together. I was sitting on Lord Snowdon's right and Princess Margaret was at the next table, with her back towards us, so I was virtually sitting between them. Lord Snowdon was very good company, and I was thoroughly enjoying myself. We were talking about the play, and he was intrigued by the severed head which comes on at the end of Macbeth, and asked if he could see it. One of the stage managers went to get it, and very discreetly handed it to him. It was quite the most grotesque thing you can imagine. It was so incredibly lifelike, or perhaps deathlike would be more appropriate! The skull was bashed in, the hair was matted with dried blood, one eye was out of its socket and lay on the cheek while the jugular vein was covered in congealed blood. Lord Snowdon thought it had been brilliantly constructed, and then he obviously had an idea. He asked me to move my chair back a little, which would allow him to lean over and touch Princess Margaret on the shoulder, which he did, and said, 'Darling, do you think it's time to go home?'

Before she had time to turn round he put the severed head in front of his own, so that when she did turn she was faced with this ghastly apparition. She looked at it for a long moment, then said, 'Tony, are you feeling quite well?' and turned back to her own table. I was filled with admiration. When it comes to social situations it is impossible to faze our royal family!

5

ON TO SOHO

After what had been a most enjoyable and interesting time at Watford, Vincent insisted that I move into his flat, which I did. Life was going to be quite different from now on, that much I knew, and I had a feeling that I was playing with fire, but it would be an adventure, and I must admit that I thrive on the unknown!

I had told Graham what the situation was when I met Vincent, and he quite understood. He wished me well, but added that if things became difficult, I was to come straight home to Aberdeen. He was just too wonderful for words.

Before I had time to settle in, Vincent had got me the part of the leading lady in a new play at Worthing Rep, so what with the commuting to Worthing and the rehearsals I scarcely had time to unpack. That play at Worthing was quite my unhappiest time in the theatre. I think the man who ran the company was called Melville Gillam. He did the casting, and apparently was noted for not reading the scripts too carefully.

At the first day's readthrough I was both surprised and delighted to discover I would be playing opposite Gerry Davis. Delighted because Gerry and I had worked together with the Whatmore Company. I liked Gerry very much, he was always fun to have around – but it surprised me that he had been cast in the part of a tall handsome Englishman. Gerry is very pleasant-

44

looking, but he is certainly not tall and would never be able to convince anyone that he was a typical Englishman. I could see the producer was as taken aback as I was, and at the coffee break he was seen marching into Melville Gillam's office with a face like thunder. It turned out that Melville had read one of the lines, 'He drove her down from London', and thought he was casting a chauffeur! He was looking for a character actor and chose Gerry.

That was just the beginning of the whole wretched business. Things might not have been so bad had the play been any good, but it was dreadful, really awful. This was its first production and unfortunately it was written by a friend of mine, who shall be nameless! He had been a producer with the Whatmore Company and we had met several times in London. He had written a delightful comedy which he himself produced in Aberdeen, and we had loved playing in it. If only he had stayed with comedy! This travesty of a play was sheer melodrama although it was meant to be a thriller. The other problem was the producer, Malcolm Farquhar, although I could sympathise with him. He had been with the same leading lady, the lovely Jan Hargreaves, for some considerable time, and they must have enjoyed working together, and now Gerry was replacing his leading man. Malcolm was not happy.

Inevitably the first night arrived, and we did our very best, we really did, but how I wished it was the last night and not the first. When it was finally over there was a rather subdued party in the bar. Malcolm made a speech, probably to exonerate himself, and told us that without his leading man and without Jan, he had felt as though he was directing with both hands tied behind his back. Not the most tactful way of putting things but I understood what he meant.

I had been to Worthing once before. In Vincent's office one day he had an SOS call from Melville, to say that they were putting on a new play by Bill Corlett, starring Dame Sybil

Thorndike, and one of the actresses had taken ill and couldn't appear that night. A script was on its way to him and would he please find someone who could learn the part on the way to Worthing, go straight into rehearsal and appear that night.

Thus I found myself on the train, looking at a much larger part than I had expected. It's the sort of situation that, if you thought about it, you would never agree to! With adrenalin pumping, I set to learn the part. As I mentioned earlier I was lucky to be a quick study but this was really pushing it! I took a taxi to the theatre, and found the cast waiting for me onstage. The producer, whose name I can't remember, marked all the moves in my script, and we were off. It is a lot easier when you are getting your cues from other actors, rather than just reading from a script. I got through the first scene all right and realised that as the character I was playing seemed to have numerous exits and entrances, with luck I could 'wing' it. That means that every time you come offstage you grab the script and learn only the lines for your next entrance, which is very much easier than being onstage all the time.

We finished the rehearsal and Dame Sybil came over for a chat. She was just enchanting. I had always heard that she was charming but to be on the receiving end of that charm was quite overwhelming. To listen to her you would never think anyone had ever had to learn a part quickly, she was just so very kind; and I was grateful to have the opportunity to meet her, even if it was under rather stressful circumstances. I will never forget her. When we left each other I found an empty dressing room to start work on the script, and by now, mainly because of Dame Sybil, I was beginning to feel a little confident. After all I had got through the rehearsal without needing a prompt and there was still more than an hour to go before the curtain went up. I can only have been studying for about ten minutes when there was a knock at the door, and in came the stage manager looking extremely embarrassed.

'I don't know how to tell you, but the girl who is playing the part has just phoned to say that she has made a miraculous recovery, and will be able to appear tonight.'

I didn't say anything. All I could think of was the dash to the station to catch the train to Worthing, then trying to learn the script before I arrived there, rehearsing with the full company, and now studying the script in order to be word perfect, and it had all been a waste of time.

I was so glad to get back to Vincent and pour out the kind of day it had been. He was very reassuring and told me that this situation was not at all unusual. Very often actresses, and presumably actors as well, felt they were sometimes not appreciated enough, and would blame flu or a virus for preventing them appearing. The idea being that whoever took over the part would be so awful that the producer would welcome back with open arms the actress who had been so sadly incapacitated. However, if it looked as though her part could easily be taken by someone else, she was out of her bed like a shot!

Vincent and I were now settling into a pattern of living which I found very exciting. He was incredibly possessive and if you were his partner you had to be with him 24 hours a day. So, the morning began with our crossing the road to Greek Street to go to his office, which was all of three minutes from his flat. There, he had decided that I should take over cabaret bookings. There could not have been anything with more glamour than going to the top nightclubs, and I just hope Vincent enjoyed it as much as I did. To me it was a world I had never known, and I loved it.

It didn't take long for me to realise that Vincent was a workaholic. He couldn't bear to be away from the office, and weekends were anathema to him. We always left London on a Friday night, sometimes going to a lovely hotel in Bournemouth, which I think was called the Clifton. It was either that or one of Vincent's houses in Dorset. He had a lot of property there and employed a full-time builder who would move in and renovate the new house, which was then sold, and Vincent would buy another. He always wanted to keep an eye on things and at least it filled in some of his hated weekends.

One Sunday morning when we were staying in Bournemouth, he suddenly said, 'Let's go somewhere different for lunch today.'

'What a lovely idea,' I said, 'Where did you have in mind?'

'Bruges,' he replied.

'*Bruges?*'

'Yes, I've always wanted to go there.' And so we did! In what seemed like no time at all we were sitting in a Belgian square enjoying the sun and a delicious lunch of the most tender steak, and crisp salad, accompanied by some very good red wine, and finished off, naturally, with Belgian chocolates.

We decided we just had time to go on one of the canal boats before flying back to London and I am so very glad we did. Somehow being on the canals meant you could see right into the heart of the city. It's called the City of Bridges after the first bridge or Brug which was built over an inlet. It still has the city walls and some wonderful Gothic buildings. Perhaps because it was a Sunday the canal banks were thronged with people just strolling and chatting, and watching the canal boats go by.

Vincent and I were in the prow of the boat and as we passed I was aware of people turning to each other and pointing and then shouting something we couldn't make out. Hardly surprising, as we didn't speak the language! I had no idea what it was all about. Had we broken some local law? But the natives seemed very friendly! Very friendly indeed and now they were all waving. At last it dawned on me. Vincent was sitting on their side of the boat and, as I mentioned earlier, he was the image of Frederick. They couldn't see my face very well, but as I had long blonde hair, I suppose that was enough, so for an hour or so we thoroughly enjoyed being Nina and Frederick and happily waved back.

Fortunately we just had time to go into The Church of Notre

Dame to see Michelangelo's statue of The Virgin and Child – I wouldn't have missed that for anything. All in all, quite an eventful afternoon.

On Monday we were back at our desks, Vincent working like mad and loving every minute of it, me having very little to do but still enjoying it. Lunch was usually the same, wonderful fresh crusty bread with thick slices of home-made pâté – a rough French pâté, the best I have ever tasted. We bought this at a charcuterie in Old Compton Street just round the corner from Greek Street and they were made as you ordered them. That, with a couple of apples, some cheese, and a glass of wine would keep us going until we went out at night. We never took more than 20 minutes to eat at lunchtime. Longer than that, and Vincent would get twitchy to get out of the flat and back to the office.

That afternoon though was going to be different. On my desk was a message to phone an Aberdeen number. When I rang it, I was put through to Grampian TV, where someone in the news department told me that Graham had had an accident playing football in a charity match and had badly damaged the cartilage in his knee. He was in a leg plaster in Foresterhill Hospital. When I told Vincent about it, at first, he was very sympathetic, but when I said it meant I would have to go back to Aberdeen he went berserk, shouting, swearing and throwing things, especially a new radio, which Graham had given me for my birthday. It was smashed to smithereens. Then he screamed at me, 'And where are you going to sleep?'

I tried to be very calm, and said, 'Probably in the guest room, but what does that matter, you know perfectly well that Graham and I don't have a sexual relationship any more.'

And then he hit me. All his height and weight were behind that punch. It sent me flying to the far end of the room, and as I lay there trying to get my breath back I almost smiled to myself, 'Well, if you will get yourself into an affair with a certified psychopath, what can you expect?'

I got up from the floor and went into the bedroom where I phoned for a taxi. I was aware that the extension phone had been lifted, so I was careful not to say exactly where I was going. I was pretty sure Vincent would assume I would go to the airport, but the thought of going out to Heathrow, and hanging around there waiting for a plane, only to arrive in the dark of the early hours in Aberdeen didn't appeal to me at all. Instead I hoped to be lucky enough to book a sleeper all the way. Suddenly the one thing in the world I wanted was a safe and peaceful night's sleep. I packed a small case, and let myself out of the flat very quietly. There was no sign of Vincent.

My luck was in, and I managed to get a First-Class sleeper. Only after I had undressed, washed, and got into bed could I allow myself to think about what had just happened.

I had never been hit by a man, either before or since, but it had taught me a lesson – never argue with a psychopath. Early on in our affair, Vincent said it was only fair to warn me that he was certified. At that time I didn't believe him. Now, I did!

All that mattered now was that I was going back to look after Graham. There was no one else to care for him, and I knew he would have done the same for me. The future would have to take care of itself, and with that I took my Lillian Beckwith book out of my case and settled down to read a few chapters.

As you probably know, Miss Beckwith was a retired school teacher who went to live in a croft in a tiny village in the Hebrides. She called it 'Bruach', and her description of the quiet way of life there, of the hills, the sheep and the sea, would calm any turbulent mind, and as for the villagers, in a very short time you felt as if you had known them all your life, and the gentle comedy running all the way through the book was a guarantee of a good night's sleep. With that in mind, I switched off the light.

I could only have been asleep for about five minutes when I was awakened by a commotion in the corridor, and amid all the shouting that was going on, I recognised Vincent's voice. Again he had gone wild, but this time he was being held by two burly guards.

'Do you know this man?' one of them asked. Rubbing my jaw ruefully, I said that I did. 'He has been causing a lot of trouble.'

I said that I could see that and suggested they took him to my compartment where I would try to calm him down, but I asked them to promise to make sure he got off the train before it left London.

When I closed the door and we were alone, Vincent burst into hysterical sobs. I knew he was beyond reason, so I just held him, and let him cry himself out. When he eventually had, he said that either he was staying on the train until it reached Aberdeen or he would throw himself under it. Ignoring the melodrama, I changed the subject by asking how he found me, because on the phone I hadn't mentioned a destination, and I was sure he would think I was at Heathrow. But apparently, when he heard me ask for a taxi, he had gone downstairs, got one for himself, and just sat there waiting for me to come out, and then followed.

Now all he could say was, '*Why* can't I come with you?'

It was then I played my trump card – 'What would happen to the office if you weren't there? You know you don't delegate, you like to do everything yourself. And if you weren't there during the week the office would fall apart.' By now he was calmer and could see the point. I told him that I would phone him whenever I got to Aberdeen and that if Graham was well enough to come home during the week, then, if Vincent still wanted to, he would be welcome to stay for the weekend. He seemed to like the idea very much, and when the guards came to escort him off the train, there was no trouble.

I was the one who lay awake wondering what on earth I had let Graham and myself in for! Vincent arrived on the first evening flight from London on the Friday. He greeted me with an enthusiasm which must have surprised anyone in Aberdeen airport who knew me! Although he only had hand luggage, he insisted on going to the carousel, where we waited for a few minutes before he pounced on a very long and unwieldy package. Seeing my puzzled expression, he said: 'It's a present. I didn't want to arrive empty-handed.'

'But what on earth is it?' I said. 'It looks most peculiar.'

And he said, 'It's a pair of oars.'

'Why ever are you bringing oars to Aberdeen?'

And he said, 'Well, you told me that you had bought Graham a Mirror dinghy, and I used to have one the same but I never learned how to sail it, so I gave it away but somehow I kept the oars and I thought Graham might like them as a spare set.'

'What a good idea,' I said without much enthusiasm. As I drove towards the house I realised that for the first time I was approaching the Northern lights of old Aberdeen with trepidation. Vincent on the other hand seemed perfectly happy and relaxed. I envied him.

The house Graham and I had in Aberdeen was a modern semi-detached villa, with the usual through lounge which could be divided into the dining room and lounge. We had not divided it, so there were two doors one in the centre and another at the far end. When Graham came home from hospital I had put a divan in the front window where he slept.

But now came the moment of introduction. Vincent, always one to make an entrance, chose the far-away door, and while I looked on, he strode, looking more like a Viking than ever, with one hand outstretched, and the other firmly holding the oars.

'I thought you might like these, Graham,' he said as they shook hands. I suddenly had an uncontrollable urge to burst out laughing, because it reminded me of the old joke about the Cambridge rowing blue who left the church after his wedding under an arch of oars, which left two bystanders very puzzled. One said to the other, 'What's them?' A friend replied, 'Them's oars.' 'Nah them's not whores, them's bridesmaids.'

Vincent came to Aberdeen every weekend until Graham was fit enough to go back to Grampian TV and then the tables turned. Graham came to London to stay with us in Soho! Not by any means every weekend, but now and then. It was all very circumspect. The three of us, when we were all together, always slept in separate bedrooms! That was no problem in Aberdeen, but Vincent's flat was smaller, so guess where I slept? Of course, in my usual habitat – the attic!

6

AN AURA FOR IRENE HANDL

Life returned to normal for Vincent and me, if you can ever call living in Soho normal! I must say I had come to enjoy it very much indeed and like so many other places, it was only when the shopkeepers began to know that you really lived there, that you were accepted, and could look on them as friends.

It was a very busy life. We would get up at nine in the morning and get to the office at ten, then Vincent would be totally immersed in phone calls, while I was in charge of booking artistes for commercials and cabaret. At lunchtime we would go back to the flat, then return to the office for the afternoon and leave work around seven in time to dress for the evening.

We never ever spent an evening in the flat. Vincent was quite incapable of relaxing – as long as he was awake he had to be working – so each night we would go to the theatre, a chore I found most enjoyable!

After the theatre, we would go on to a nightclub for our evening meal, but we were really there to see the cabaret artistes, in case Vincent spotted someone he would like sign up. Eventually we would get back to bed around three in the morning, if we were lucky, to have a few hours' sleep before the alarm went off.

I did some television work but nothing of any importance, and I was more than delighted to turn down an invitation to spend a season at Worthing, as their leading lady!

Nonetheless, I was beginning to long for some theatre work, so when Vincent opened his mail one morning and said, 'How do you feel about auditioning for *The Mousetrap*?,' I told him I would love to, though secretly I thought it would be just too good to be true if I did get the part. I knew the contracts were all for one year, which is a long time in the West End, but best of all the production was on at the Ambassador Theatre, which was, at the most, five minutes walk from the flat, and eight minutes from the office.

It couldn't have been more convenient, but I was very unsure of London auditions, because a very short time before this I had both won and lost a part in the West End. It was a comedy thriller, one of the Mrs Puffin plays, Mrs Puffin of course being played by the star actress Irene Handl. The part being recast was the younger leading lady, for the play was to go on tour and the actress who had done the play in London didn't want to tour with it.

I had gone to the audition, and as usual, when I saw the other actresses who were up for the part, thought I had no chance, but when I read the script I began to think I really could play the character; after all, it was comedy! When we had all read for the director, three of us were asked to stay, and the others left. We knew that now a great discussion was going on as to who would be cast, but we just chatted, and it really was very pleasant. After a very short time the stage manager came in and called one of us into the office. That left the remaining actress and myself bewildered. Were we in the running, or were we about to be sent home? A few minutes later the other actress was also called into the office, and I was on my own. I was determined to be positive, and told myself this was my first audition for the West End, and it hadn't been all that frightening, so hopefully there would be more plays to try for.

At that point the director came in and said they were very

happy to offer me the part, if I was agreeable, and was willing to go on tour. To both questions I said a delighted YES! A moment later the stage manager returned, said she was so glad I was joining the company and she had only one question – what was my dress size? When I said size ten, she beamed, and said, 'Yes, I thought so.'

When she and the director went into the office, presumably to work out contract details, I was extremely glad to be on my own.

So much for positive thinking – I was dreaming that they had thought I had a real talent for comedy whereas the only reason I had been chosen was that I fitted the clothes! That would save them a great deal of money, but it did nothing for my self-confidence! I was given a ticket for that evening's performance with the promise that at the end of the play I should meet Irene Handl in her dressing room. I really looked forward to that. I had seen her so often in films and on television and thought her wonderfully warm comedy was admirable.

It really felt quite strange, watching a play which I was going to be in the following week, and noting particularly the actress from whom I was to take over, but I thoroughly enjoyed both her performance and the play itself, and needless to say, the audience loved Irene Handl.

I had to wait some time to see Miss Handl because there were so many of the stage staff and management going in and out of her room. I began to wonder if something had gone wrong that night, but then for all I knew, it was just their way of looking after a rather elderly star. When I was ushered into her room I must confess I was taken aback by her. Instead of the warm, lovable comedienne I had expected there was a lady who was obviously annoyed about something, and didn't want to be bothered with a replacement actress. Her face and her eyes were absolutely icy. I began to feel the chill before we had even spoken and the first words she said to me were, 'We have met before.'

To which I could only reply, 'No, I'm sorry Miss Handl, we have not.'

'Rubbish,' she said, 'I have talked to you before.'

'Miss Handl, I promise you if I had had the pleasure of meeting you, I certainly would have remembered it.'

She gazed at me for some time, and said, '*You* may have forgotten, but I never forget an aura and I know I have met your aura before.'

There is just no answer to that, is there? The only polite move I could make was to remove myself and my aura from her room. As I expected, Vincent got a phone call the next morning to say that with the regret of the director, I would no longer be needed on tour with Miss Handl. I learned later that it took a very long time before Irene Handl found someone with a satisfactory aura, but I was very relieved to be out of that production.

Now I was to audition for *The Mousetrap*, but how different this was. For a start, the stage manager sent me a script which meant I could study it and learn the lines of the scene they were going to rehearse, and best of all, I realised that I had worked with the director before, in Aberdeen. He was the charming 'Slim' Ramsden. He and his lovely wife Christine were always a joy to be around. His real name was Dennis, but some years earlier the Whatmore Players had been invited to put on one of their productions at Balmoral for the royal family. It went very well, and the cast was invited to stay behind and be presented. Unfortunately the producer who was making the introductions lost his nerve when he reached Dennis and for the life of him couldn't remember his first name, but after a pause, he said, with great aplomb, 'This is Slim Ramsden, your Majesty,' and Slim he was from that day on.

It was lovely to see him again, and it certainly didn't make me nervous for the audition. Naturally I had dressed for my part of Miss Casewell, who was an exceedingly butch lady, and it was a very busy morning. When I left the theatre after the audition at 11.30am I had to go straight to the BBC where Vincent was waiting for me. We were to attend a celebration lunch given for Jessie Matthews, one of Vincent's clients, to mark her success as Mrs Dale in *Mrs Dale's Diary* on radio. These parties were always splendid, because there would be so many friends you hadn't seen for years. One of them was chatting to Vincent and asked him, 'I've been told there is a new woman in your life, is that true?'

Vincent agreed that was indeed so, but when asked if she was an actress, he said, 'No, she's a long-distance lorry driver'.

Right on cue I appeared, wearing my butch audition clothes of cord trousers, boots, a heavy checked shirt and a sheepskin jacket.

Vincent's friend was heard to say, 'Good Lord, she really *is* a lorry driver!'

The next day to the delight of both of us, Vincent got a phone call to say that I had been chosen for the part of Miss Casewell. He turned the entire day and night into total celebration and we had a wonderful time – the result being that it really wasn't until the following day that I realised what a momentous decision had been made for me.

I was no longer a free agent. I was now absolutely committed to spending the year in London. I could only hope that Graham had given up playing football, and wasn't going to be accident-prone! I also realised that I would have to make a quick visit to Aberdeen. I had come down to London with a reasonable wardrobe of clothes but there was no way they would be enough to last for a year, and I would have to collect the outfit I was going to wear in *The Mousetrap*.

There was a rather odd financial arrangement about that. We would provide the clothes we were going to wear in the production and the management paid us a very generous sum of money for them, and if we still wanted to keep them when we left the production, we could buy them back for next to nothing!

It was very strange to return to Aberdeen. I had travelled by overnight sleeper again, and Graham very kindly met me at the station and drove me to his new home, in the fishing village of Portlethan, just a few miles south of Aberdeen. The village, which was built on the cliff top, looked delightful and all the cottages looked so fresh with their whitewash and painted doors and windows. Graham's were painted a pretty pale blue, and his house had the advantage of a garage built on by the previous owner. Every mod con, I began to think, until I discovered that the only lavatory in the whole place was a makeshift cubicle in the garage! It also contained all the garden tools and a coalhouse, all very necessary, but certainly no room for a car.

Graham had told me previously that he wanted to sell our house and move out of town. I couldn't blame him – I think if I had stayed in Aberdeen we would have sold it earlier. Graham's problem was that the house was in our joint names and he needed me to sign the papers. I think he knew there would be no difficulty in that, and when he told me he had found a cottage he really liked I was just so happy for him, and when I saw it I couldn't have agreed more with him. It was happily quaint, very, very peaceful, and yet with friendly neighbours to pass the time of day, and the view from the glassed-in veranda in front of the cottage looked out over the beach and then over the sea, forever, with nothing on the horizon except sky. It was a view I would recall many, many times in London.

I had to return there the same day because rehearsals for *The Mousetrap* began the following morning, and this time, to be on the safe side, I was flying back. At this time, in 1964, flying to London from Aberdeen meant changing planes at Edinburgh airport. I rather like flying. There is a sense of freedom in that no one can write to you or phone you. Your luggage is on board, but you won't see it again until you arrive, so what is there to do except take out the good book you've been saving, lean back and enjoy it? I had done that on the journey to Edinburgh and sat in the lounge now looking forward to continuing it on my way to London. There was only a short time to go before boarding, when an announcement came over the Tannoy. It seemed there was fog at Heathrow and no planes could land. Well it was the end of October after all, but what did I say about not seeing your luggage until you arrived?

The next scenario was a very disgruntled group of passengers at the carousel waiting for luggage to be retrieved. Instead of hearing soothing music, we had another announcement, saying that as there would be no planes landing at Heathrow at all that night, arrangements had been made for those of us who had to get to London to be taken to Waverley station to catch the London train. It was being held for us, so would we please make all possible speed to catch the bus which was waiting.

I would have loved to have been speedy but two things held me back – first finding a trolley, and then getting my luggage on to it (which I think would have defeated a champion weightlifter, far less me). Somehow we all boarded the train, and our luggage was stowed away. You can perhaps imagine the welcome we got from our fellow travellers, and who can blame them? There they all were, with their long reserved seats, looking forward to a pleasant journey from one capital to another and to arriving on time. To make matters worse, this was at a time when there were armrests in the compartments, all of which had to be raised to allow this motley crew to pack in and crush them to bits. The compartment I was in had only two or three passengers already there, but from now on it was going to be shoulder to shoulder for many hours.

We were all so miserable that we didn't even talk to each other. Those of us beside a window stared out as though fascinated by the trucks of coal we could see, while those unfortunate enough not to have such a stimulating view could only stare at the floor.

I wondered what was holding us back now, when there was

an announcement on the train's loudspeaker. It was from the airport, saying that the fog had cleared at Heathrow and our flight was back on schedule. Those who wished to resume the flight should join the airport bus at Waverley station. Instant pandemonium.

Practically all of the compartment jumped to their feet. Cases, bags, and heaven knows what rained down from the luggage racks, and if they didn't land on our toes the owners did! I had only two options. Either I followed the madding crowd, and hauled down my impossibly heavy luggage and dragged it all the way to the bus, or, I could take off my shoes and put my feet up on the now empty seat in front of me, use my lovely warm coat as a blanket and sleep until I reached London. Being of a naturally idle disposition, there was no contest! Within two minutes I was fast asleep.

I wakened just as we approached London and felt grateful that I only had a short taxi drive to Shaftesbury Avenue. A friendly guard appeared and was kind enough to get my luggage down from the rack and put it on a trolley on the platform. I was so grateful to him, not only for his strength, but also for his rather fatherly advice. When I thanked him, he put his arm round my shoulder, and said, 'Take care of yourself today – try and have a rest.' What a strange thing to say, I thought, as I joined the queue for taxis. I was looking around at adverts on the station walls as you do when there's nothing else to look at, when I suddenly saw a newspaper billboard – 'Plane Crash at Heathrow. No survivors!' It could only have been the Edinburgh plane. It was.

Now I understood what the kind railway guard had meant. He understood how those of us who had stayed on the train would feel when we learned of the tragic accident.

I think I was in a state of shock for quite a while, then my first reaction was the memory of all the business men who had trampled on my feet in their wild dash to get to the airport. If only they had missed the bus that was waiting for them, I would gladly have had my feet trampled on their return. Mercifully it must have been an instant death for them, because the plane crash landed on the runway, but the thought of all the wives and families having the dreadful news told to them was heart-breaking.

I was told the press only mentioned two who hadn't boarded the plane, the Duke of Buccleuch and an actress going to London to appear in *The Mousetrap*.

I arrived at the flat around seven in the morning, and let myself in very quietly. Vincent was fast asleep, so I went into the kitchen and made a coffee. Sitting at the table with my hands clasped around a warming mug, I reflected on the day. From Graham to Vincent, from Aberdeen to Edinburgh, and then a random choice between life and death.

The only conclusion I could come to was that from this day on, every day of my life would be a bonus, and for that I must be grateful.

7

TAMING OF THE SHREW

The first day of rehearsal went extremely smoothly, as did everything to do with *The Mousetrap*, but then they had a great deal of experience! The two members of the cast who had been with the production for many years, David Raven and Mysie Monte, could not have been more helpful, or more welcoming. Mysie, I believe, came from a theatrical family, because as a very young child she had sat on the knee of Sir Henry Irving. He had been trying to console her on the death of her mother, but shortly afterwards he, himself, died. It seems that at his funeral the toddler Mysie was heard to say, 'Oh Daddy, how dreadful, first Mummy, and now Irving.' A great deal for a small child to cope with.

Our first night went well, and everything settled into a regular pattern. I had wondered if I would still be expected to work in the office in the mornings, but of course I was!

Shortly after I arrived in London, I had yet another name change. I had always disliked the name Audrey. To me, it conjured up two different pictures: one was the nasty girl in all the children's school stories and the other was a very tatty hairdresser's in Maryhill Road! The problem was to choose a new name. It isn't easy, because apart from the choice itself, there is a feeling of guilt about rejecting your parents' choice. I eventually got it down to two names which I liked – Jane and

Kate. Jane I eventually ditched because it was too bland with Matheson, whereas Kate was plain and straightforward, and I'd always thought I was a bit of a Shrew, and certainly deserved to be Tamed . . . So, with my thanks to Shakespeare, I legally became Kate Matheson.

Being in a play didn't really make a difference to our way of life at all. The office in the morning, back to the flat for a quick lunch, office in the afternoon, and then at 6.30 Vincent would walk me round to the theatre. And at the end of the play he would be waiting in the wings when I came offstage. We would then go to the nightclubs, a bit later than we used to, but that was the only change. I was thoroughly enjoying it all, though Christmas was a little difficult to fit in!

Vincent went into the New Year with all sorts of resolutions, and first on his list was our getting married. He was determined that Graham and I should divorce as soon as possible. It took quite some time to get a divorce in those days so Vincent knew he would have to wait years. Nonetheless, when we left to go to the office the following morning, I was startled when he hailed a cab and dragged me into it.

'What on earth are you doing?' I asked.

He smiled, 'You'll see.'

We arrived at a very plush reception area where a beautiful and immaculate young woman said, 'Mr Shaw, we've been looking forward to seeing you. Please will you both have a seat, Mr Stonely will be with you in just a few minutes.'

I stared at Vincent. 'These are lawyers' offices, aren't they? Why are we here?'

'Because, dearest Kate, you are going to change your name.'

'Not *again*,' I laughed. 'Not on your life.'

'I'm perfectly serious,' he said sternly. 'I know it will be some time before we can actually get married, but there is no reason why you can't change your name to mine today. From now on your name will be Kate Matheson Shaw.'

64

I stood up very calmly and spoke quietly, so that only he could hear. 'I'm very sorry, Vincent, but you never mentioned this before, and we have had no chance to discuss it. I have no intention of changing my name whatsoever.' And I left.

The drive back to the office was made in total silence. Once there all hell broke loose. Nobody could do anything right, especially me. Books were thrown on the floor, files were swept off his desk, and heaven help anyone who had the temerity to phone that day!

To my surprise he still walked with me to the theatre, without a word being said.

In the peace and quiet of my own room, which I was beginning to think of as my sanctuary, I thought in great depth about what had happened that day. My first reaction was to feel sorry for Vincent – he had obviously thought it would a lovely surprise and I'm pretty sure he had a celebration lunch planned and a party back at the office later on. Instead, it had all gone wrong, and he was very hurt and extremely angry. What was more difficult to analyse was my own reaction to his idea. The truth, when I eventually arrived at it, was startling. I didn't want to marry Vincent, not ever. I was very fond of him, but I certainly wasn't in love with him. We had got off to an incredibly exciting start, it felt like nought to 60mph in five seconds! Quite an impossible situation to sustain, and for me, the flaws were getting more, and bigger, each day.

I was amazed when the play ended to find Vincent not only in the wings, but smiling! I wondered if he, too, had done a lot of heart searching that evening. We went out together for supper, had a most enjoyable time, and even loved the cabaret. The visit to the lawyer was never mentioned, but the one difference was that from then on Vincent always referred to me as his wife, and always introduced me to friends and strangers as such.

I didn't like it, I felt uncomfortable, and decided there had to be a showdown in the very near future. I wanted to have it there and then, but for some reason I just couldn't find the energy.

That was when I realised for the first time that I didn't feel at all well, and hadn't done so for some time.

The following week, onstage during a scene in which all the action and dialogue took place on the other side of the stage, I was sitting on a sofa when an actor behind me whispered, 'Did you know you have lumps on one side of your neck?' I resisted the temptation to find out if that were true until I got back to my dressing room. Sure enough I had small lumps going from my shoulder to my hairline.

When I mentioned it to Vincent, I was immediately packed off to Harley Street where I saw a most unpleasant Irish doctor who thought he was God's gift to women. Why are they always the ones you wouldn't look at twice? After he had examined me and taken blood samples, I asked him for his opinion, 'Very difficult to say, we'll have to wait for the lab results, but I would think it's either non-specific, or it's glandular fever or leukaemia. Good morning.'

Totally charmed by his bedside manner, I made my way back to the office. Vincent was as puzzled as I was about the possible diagnosis, but I could sense he was also very worried. The last thing he needed in his life was an invalid! That night he flew into a flaming temper about the time I spent sending Graham tapes, and even worse, the time I spent listening to his. I was so tired and miserable that all I could do was ask him if we could talk about that, and a great many other things, in the morning.

When I got up in the morning I made us coffee, and we had an amazingly calm and sensible discussion.

I told him we had reached a turning-point, and that to give us both some space I was going to move out of his flat that afternoon. 'Why?' was all he said.

So I told him the truth, as I saw it. 'You and I embarked on a crazy romance. It was so hot, it had to burn itself out; we couldn't possibly have lived at that pace for long, and now it's probably time to accept that. There was a long pause, and when he spoke it sounded like a stranger talking. He was kind, understanding and very reasonable. He wanted to know where I was going to live, and I told him a girlfriend with her own flat had a spare room to let, and that was where I would be staying. He knew the girl I was talking about, Ann, and approved, and then he just talked. It was lovely. He said how much our affair had meant to him and that he was sure neither of us would forget it. How right he was!

I was so grateful that we had both realised the parting of the ways at the same time. I never saw him again. We had to have business phone calls, but that was all.

When I went to Harley Street for the result of my tests, the doctor was in a much better mood, but when he saw me he said, 'What's happened to you? You look really ill.'

'Perhaps you know more than I do, after all you have the results.' He looked at me vaguely, and began to shuffle through some papers on his desk. After a time he looked up and said, 'Oh yes, I remember, it was non-specific.' I asked him what exactly that meant, and he said, 'Could be anything.' With that expert medical knowledge, I left, feeling more ill than ever.

I went back to Vincent's flat and packed. I had thought I would feel some regrets, but on the contrary I felt a sense of freedom.

It was short-lived! When I arrived at Ann's flat she apologised that the room I was to have had no carpet. It was a fairly small room, so I suggested I should give her the money for a new one. This she gladly accepted, and while we were chatting, told me that there would be three of us in the flat, not just ourselves. She had fallen madly in love with a man who was a great deal younger than herself, and he was now living with her. I tried to ignore the alarm bells that were ringing in my head. Perhaps this boy Pete would make her very happy. I certainly hoped so.

That was until I met him! He was a very handsome young

man, and well aware of it, always with a captivating smile, and oozing charm, but when the smile was no longer necessary, the eyes were quite unbelievably cold and calculating.

Ann, being of an impulsive nature, wanted to buy the carpet that afternoon, so collecting Pete from their room, off they went with the money I had given Ann.

I spent the afternoon unpacking, feeling decidedly dismal. Nothing seemed to be going right. I was convinced that leaving Vincent was the only answer for both of us, though I was sure he would not be alone for any length of time. Twenty-four hours, if that, would be his limit!

Ann arrived back much earlier than I expected, looking slightly flushed, but very happy. She told me they had had a wonderful time shopping, and had gone to a wine bar on the way home. I told her how happy I was for her, not only for the afternoon, but that she had found someone who made her feel so marvellous. It was nearly time for me to leave for the theatre, so I asked her if she had found a carpet she liked for the spare room.

'Oh, yes, I meant to tell you, Pete saw the money you had given me, and on the way to buy it, we passed a shoe shop and he spotted a pair of shoes he said he couldn't live without. They are simply gorgeous but unbelievably expensive, so I'm afraid the carpet will have to wait.'

I got on the tube to Charing Cross for the theatre, and thought, it must be me, everything is falling about me. I've ended a relationship, I'm being ripped off in the place where I stay, and I feel more ill than ever.

I had never been so glad to arrive at my dressing-room sanctuary, to find the loveliest card from Sybil Thorndike to the owner of the dressing room of which she had the use during the day. Apparently she was rehearsing for a production of *Arsenic and Old Lace*, which starred Sybil Thorndike, her husband Lewis Casson and Athene Seyler.

The management of the production were extremely worried

about the safety of Athene Seyler. She absolutely refused to accept the chauffeur-driven car they provided for her, insisting on travelling on the top deck of the bus where she could enjoy the view! Everyone was so afraid that, as an elderly lady, she might have a bad fall coming down the stairs. Enter the solution – Mr and Mrs Casson to the rescue!

Sybil Thorndike went to Athene Seyler and begged a favour. She said that she was very concerned about her husband Lewis, it seemed that he had become abnormally afraid of the London traffic, and although she did her best to reassure him, it would be so much easier if she had a friend to help. Would Athene be kind enough to travel with them in their car, instead of taking the bus? Athene, always happy to help, agreed.

Problem solved.

I wished mine had been too. Before I had put on my make-up, the stage manager looked in as usual, to check we were all present and correct, and seeing me, said, 'Good God, are you OK?' When I told him that I didn't feel all that good, he wrote down the address of a doctor and demanded that I go and see him in the morning.

This of course I did. The doctor turned out to be a friendly, avuncular GP. He examined me and said, 'You've had a report from Harley Street, I believe. I shall send for it, and whenever it arrives I shall send it with my own diagnosis to your production company, with advice that you should be released from your contract as soon as possible. I would also give you my personal advice. You should leave London for somewhere peaceful, if that is possible.'

The only place I could go to was Aberdeen, and when I phoned Graham to ask if that would be possible, he couldn't have been kinder, and even insisted on coming down to London to take me back. I was given permission to leave the following weekend. It was a stroke of luck that the 'Miss Casewell' from whom I had taken over was an actress I had worked with in plays in London. Fortunately she was free, and happy to return to *The Mousetrap*.

The drive back from London felt very strange. My car was in a mews garage, which Vincent owned. (He always left his car at his parents' home in Lancing. He wasn't too happy driving, nor were the other drivers on the same road as him!) His garage was next to Enoch Powell's, a most interesting man in the papers and on television, but to a 'Good morning, Mr Powell' outside his garage, the reply was just a grunt. And who could blame him, he had a world to put to rights.

Leaving London was such a muddle of emotions – the excitement of being there and of booking artistes for cabaret, and generally just being involved in a side of show business I had never known before. And most of all my affair with Vincent. I didn't regret that. It was a shattering experience, one I would never forget, but it had burned itself out and now I was going back to Portlethen for its wonderful peace, as my doctor ordered.

I was so blessed to have someone like Graham, who is the kindest of men, though we both knew I would be off again, heaven knew where or when . . .

When we arrived at the cottage I didn't go in straight away. I just wanted to breathe the clearest air I had had for some time.

Graham's caring and the calming effect of the sea outside the window convinced me that I would quickly recover. It didn't happen, so I had to go to a local doctor. What a difference from Harley Street! He had time to talk and to question. What amazed me was when he asked, 'Do you think you have got over your glandular fever, or is it still affecting you?'

I stared at him in astonishment. 'I wasn't told I had glandular fever.'

'You most certainly have, and I think you are still suffering from it, but hopefully, if you have enough rest you will shortly be free of it.'

Suddenly I realised why I had felt so ill in London, not a place in which to be ill if you were at the mercy of my Harley Street doctor!

Gradually I began to recover, and the peace of mind from receiving very few phone calls, or visitors, began to make me feel truly like a human being and not the zombie I had thought I was.

The never ending change of the sea, from storm to choppy to calm, fascinates me. I could never tire of watching the sea, and it certainly gave me back my health.

The summer was mostly sunny, and I would sit in the garden with nothing to think about other than what I would cook for Graham's evening meal. It was total peace.

8

SEALED WITH A KISS

As the summer of 1966 began to show the first signs of autumn I had a letter from Vincent, purely business of course, asking if I would like to play the Fairy Queen in *A Wish for Jamie* with Alec Finley at His Majesty's Theatre, Aberdeen? I couldn't believe it, and as I had now completely recovered, there was nothing I looked forward to more than working again, and to be with Alec who was a long-time friend was too good to be true.

Clare Richards, also a dear friend, was playing the leading fairy, Aggie Goose, which was comedy all the way through, and no one could have played it better. The Fairy Queen, on the other hand, was extremely dull, but when Alec asked me to be a 'feed' in his sketches I couldn't have been happier to do so.

A feed is someone who uses their dialogue to set up the comedian's joke and I loved doing that. Having realised that Alec was always pleased to have a happy company, and more than anything, a happy audience, I asked if the Fairy Queen could be allowed to sound like Her Majesty. Alec was all for it, and it made the winter season pass enormously quickly!

Every night Clare would join me after the performance in my dressing room, where we would relax with a glass of wine, and one night she said, 'I'm told that Rikki Fulton is coming to Aberdeen for a summer season, do you know him?'

I replied with a rather choked voice, 'Yes, I knew him a long time ago. Do you by any chance have his phone number in Glasgow?'

Of course being the organised lady she is, within a very few minutes she was back with his ex-directory number.

The following morning I phoned his number, which was answered by a woman who told me that Mr Fulton was not available, and would not be so for the following week. She didn't give me her name so I assumed she lived with him and that it would be tactless to phone again. Instead I wrote to Rikki and asked if he had already got his full company, and if not, would he consider my joining them, as I had been working in comedy with Alec Finley – though I wasn't sure if he would remember me from the days of the Giffnock Players.

By return post I got a letter from him to say that he certainly did remember me but that he was fully cast for the season. He hoped I would come to the show, and go backstage to say hello to him. My first thought was, try and stop me!

Oddly enough I didn't go round to see him when I first saw the show. My father was in Aberdeen on business, and when he learned that Rikki was at the theatre, he was determined to see the show. He had always been an avid admirer of Rikki, and they still exchanged Christmas cards after all those years. Graham was working at Grampian that night, so my father and I went on our own.

It felt like going to the *Five Past Eight Show*, though it wasn't as lavish as they used to be, but then there never has been a production to equal *Five Past Eight*. Rikki was working splendidly, despite a not over-responsive Aberdeen audience, but all I was thinking about was that after 17 years I was actually seeing him again, and my feelings for him were absolutely the same as ever, though tinged with regret that he was living with someone else. It was hardly surprising. I knew Ethel had left him, and was now in London, and he was pretty unlikely not to have a lady in his life after that.

During the interval we went to the bar and were delighted to meet Peter, a friend of Rikki's who had been in the Giffnock Theatre Players, and had kept the friendship flourishing. My father was so happy to talk about the Players, of which he was still a member. When I could get a word in, I told Peter that I had phoned Rikki but it was a woman who answered.

'Yes, that would be Mrs Wares,' and seeing my questioning look, he added, 'She's Rikki's housekeeper.' I could have kissed him.

All through the second half I could only think that in just some minutes I would be meeting him again, but then I had second thoughts. I knew that my father would want to see him, and I didn't want my first meeting with Rikki to be as Bill Craig-Brown's daughter. I know that sounds awful, but for both Rikki and myself our amateur days were over, and I wanted to meet him as a fellow professional.

When we left the theatre, my father said, 'Now, let's go and see Rikki,' to which I replied, 'Daddy, do go, but if you don't mind I'll wait for you in the car.'

He stared at me in astonishment, 'But you used to be mad about him.'

'I know,' I said, 'and I still am, but I just don't feel like seeing him tonight, and after all I have the whole summer to meet him, and you only have tonight.'

'Well, I'm not going on my own,' and no matter how much I tried to persuade him, he refused to go and eventually said, 'It's been a long day, driving up here and then doing business all afternoon. Just drive me back to the hotel.'

This I did, feeling horribly guilty. I then headed back to Portlethen. As I drove, I had very mixed feelings. Seeing Rikki had really set my head in a spin, but that had been Rikki the performer, not Rikki the man. Had I blown it? Was it a question of so near and yet so far? I would soon know – after all he was there for the whole summer.

When their programme at the theatre changed, Graham and I

went to the first night, and I can't honestly say I was concentrating on the show as much as I should have been. All I could think of was the fact that in minutes I was going to meet the man I fell in love with as a young teenager, and that I had never forgotten him. He almost certainly wouldn't recognise me, and probably wouldn't even like me. I was talking myself into total pessimism and thought that the wisest plan was just to return to Portlethen, and forget that schoolgirl dream I used to have about him.

All that was to change at the curtain call. When Rikki stepped forward to make his speech to the audience, thanking them and wishing them well, he was no longer the comedian, but the man I had fallen in love with. I asked Graham if he would mind if I went backstage, and being the lovely man he is, he said: 'Not at all, I've got some scripts I want to read in the car, so I'll be quite happy until you come back.'

I went through the stage door, and it was calming to be in a theatre I knew so well. Rikki was in the same dressing room that I had been in last time I worked at His Majesty's. It should all have been reassuring, so why did I feel like a tongue-twisted teenager. Hoping that wouldn't show, I knocked on the door. It was opened at once, and I found myself in a room crowded with people.

I could see Rikki in the far corner surrounded by what I thought were some members of the company, and many visitors. I didn't go over to him, but stayed talking to the handsome man who had opened the door for me. He was Jimmy Donald who owned the theatre – in fact in those days the Donald family owned most of Aberdeen. He was a debonair fellow with a lovely wife called Anne, and they were superb company.

As we were talking theatre, I realised that Rikki was looking at us. Our eyes met, yes, across a crowded room. I knew what mine were saying but I didn't dare guess what his were. Within seconds he was at my side, and after all the usual platitudes, he kissed me politely on the cheek. At that, Clem Ashby, who had been Rikki's feed since the *Five Past Eight* days, came over to join us, and seconds later the three men were discussing the game of golf they had played that afternoon. Quite soon, Jimmy said he would have to get home, and I was left with Rikki and Clem. After a brief conversation, I asked them both if they would like to join Graham and me for supper after the show the next night. They accepted with enthusiasm, which was because in their flat they were doing their own cooking, and neither could exactly be called cordon bleu. I promised I would make a very simple meal; not knowing either their likes or dislikes I certainly wasn't going to be adventurous.

The next morning I went in to Aberdeen to shop for our meal. I always enjoyed this, because the town had such wonderful fishmongers, butchers and bakers.

Arriving back at Portlethen was a different story though. When I started slicing the fruit for a salad, I came down to earth with a bang, and asked myself, 'What on earth do you think you are doing? You are behaving like an idiot. All right, you know it wasn't just a schoolgirl crush you had on Rikki, but he doesn't know you at all, he has never met you as an adult, and the chances are he won't even like you and it could turn out to be a most disappointing evening.'

Having given myself a sensible talking-to, I began to set the table.

Rikki and Clem arrived before eleven and we invited them into our sitting room. It was rather an interesting small room. The walls were the original stone which Graham and I had liked, so we never covered them, and our fireplace had a mantelpiece of a discarded railway sleeper! It always gave our guests something to talk about.

When Graham brought the drinks in we all sat chatting for a while and Clem and Graham were getting along famously. I asked them to excuse me while I went to cook the steaks, and headed for the kitchen. I checked the potatoes baking in the oven, another ten minutes would do them, and I had a green salad and tomatoes waiting in the fridge. I was just slicing lemons for the smoked salmon starter when I felt two arms around my waist. I couldn't believe it when I turned round to discover they belonged to Rikki. He said, 'I don't think they'll miss me, but I was missing you.' I was quite beyond speech, so he added, 'Will you come and see me tomorrow afternoon, please? We have a lot to talk about.'

When eventually I recovered the power of speech, I was able to tell him that there was nothing I would like more, and when he gave me his address it became even easier. He was just round the corner from Grampian TV.

Then we kissed, and how we kissed. After a long time we gazed at each other, and his eyes were saying the same as mine. This can't be happening, I thought – and went to call Graham and Clem through for supper.

The evening had become night, and as we all talked, night became morning! The four of us all went for a stroll down to the sea about 6.30, and then our guests departed.

Quite a bit later that morning, I did what any woman would do under the circumstances, and went to my hairdresser.

After that I had a recording to make at Grampian TV. When I had finished the Panto season with Alec Finlay I was given the chance to work as an announcer, something I'd never done before, and I enjoyed it immensely. After the recording I walked through the foyer, thinking – he is just round the corner! As I went towards the door, I met a dear friend Douglas Kynoch, a most delightful and clever writer, who at that time was the senior announcer. He looked me up and down and then said, 'What has happened to you, you look radiant!' I thought it wiser at that time not to explain the situation.

Strangely enough as I walked the short distance to the house Rikki was renting, I had no feeling of nervousness at all. If I could believe what had happened between us the night before, all I wanted was to be with him again.

He was at the front window as I approached and had the front door open before I reached it. We kissed, and then he took me into the living room, he sat in an armchair and drew me onto his knee and said, 'Will you marry me?' It didn't present a problem, so I just said, 'I thought you'd never ask.'

We talked a lot and laughed a great deal, then Rikki took me by the hand, led me into his bedroom and there we undressed and got into bed, and for the first time in my life I made love, we both did.

I know that must seem rather strange, but this was so utterly different from anything I had ever known. Every touch, every movement, was made with sheer love, and as I lay in his arms all I could think was, 'Dear God, don't let me wake up and find it has all been a dream.'

It wasn't!

We arranged to meet the following day, and as I drove away from Rikki, I knew my life would never be the same again. That probably sounds melodramatic, but it was absolutely true. This was the most important and incredible thing that had ever happened to me. If we were to spend our future together, my joy would not be contained! On the other hand we had only met three days ago, so how could we possibly have fallen in love so quickly? I knew why I had, I was programmed to love Rikki from an early age, but how could he possibly feel the same? Yet it seemed that he did feel exactly the same, and if I was wrong, then I knew I could never feel the happiness that enveloped me at that moment, ever again.

I was grateful to be alone that evening, because I don't think I could have carried on a coherent conversation with anyone, but by the time Graham came home I had reached a semblance of normality and as we had our supper we talked about the night before. Graham was saying how much he had liked Rikki, and I wondered if he guessed what was happening between Rikki and me – but if he did, he gave no indication of it. I realised that if my dream came true, and Rikki and I were going to spend our future together, then of course Graham would be the first to be told, but certainly not now, just hours after Rikki and I had met.

I went to Rikki's house the following afternoon, and again no Clem. I was beginning to wonder if he really did live there, and what Rikki had to pay to get the house to himself! By this time Rikki and I couldn't bear to be apart, and spent every possible moment together, although that wasn't very easy. At Grampian TV I was a very junior member of a team that consisted of Douglas Kynoch, a splendid man called Jimmy Spankie, who was unfailingly good-natured and very funny, and Graham, which contributed greatly to my enjoyment. I was able to tell Rikki that when I was on the late shift and closing down the station, my Good Night wishes to the viewers were really meant for him alone!

Whenever our work permitted, we were together, talking non-stop, and with endless laughter. Strangely, we didn't talk about the future, but only the here and now – neither of us could believe what had happened to us, but we wanted it to last forever.

I do remember one afternoon in which we didn't have a row, or even a cross word, but somehow we were not on the same wavelength and I went back to the cottage feeling thoroughly depressed. When I arrived there was an unfamiliar car in the driveway and inside I found Graham with unexpected guests. They were a young married couple, and the most attractive girl, Yvonne, was a distant relation of Graham's. They were touring around the Highlands from their home in Wales, but I was relieved to learn they would not be staying the night, not even for an evening meal. I felt so guilty at not feeling hospitable, but all I wanted was to crawl into bed and be thoroughly miserable. I was convinced my dream was falling apart, and if it did I didn't want to live.

I think I made a pretty pathetic afternoon tea for them, and then sat there like a silent witness until they left. Fortunately

Graham and Yvonne were busy recalling family memories and seemed to have plenty to talk to each other about.

The following day Rikki was his usual loving self, so obviously I had misconstrued our emotions. Not only was he quite wonderful, but he told me that he was going back to Glasgow for the weekend, and asked if I would join him. This invitation I was happy to accept, though with some trepidation. It really felt like the old days when you were invited home to meet Mother, or in Rikki's case Mrs Wares! What, I wondered, would happen if we didn't like each other? And I feared the worst – after all, wives were ten a penny, but housekeepers were like gold.

I drove down from Aberdeen to Glasgow in the early afternoon. Rikki had left in the morning and I suppose I expected to see him at the window, but there was no sign of life at all. I parked in the driveway of the house and rang the bell. After some time, the door was opened by a handsome young Italian man. Deciding I had obviously come to the wrong house, I apologised, and explained that I was looking for a Mr Fulton, to which the young man replied, 'He's in the kitchen, having his hair done,' and so he was, having it beautifully cut and shaped by the young man's father, Mr Johnny Ionta. Shortly after that Rikki lost touch with him. We never discovered what became of him although we tried every phone number we had. Rikki tried a few hairdressers without much success, until we found the wonderful Neil, who came to the house, and saved the day!

After the hairdressing session, Rikki had the rather daunting job of showing me over the house. I knew how much it meant to him, but the problem was that I didn't like it, and the more I saw of it the less I liked it!

When we at last finished the Grand Tour we settled in the drawing room with glasses of wine. I was very quiet. I had to think the whole situation over. Eventually I realised that it wasn't the house I disliked, it was what had been done to it. The rooms were all large, and the master bedroom was enormous, exactly the same size as the drawing room below it, but then when the house was built in 1902 it would have been the drawing room and the room below would have been the dining room. I began to feel that the potential of the house hadn't been realised, and that basically it was beautiful – what was wrong was the décor.

I didn't know how to phrase it without offending Rikki, but he was the one who spoke.

'You know how much this house means to me, but if you are willing, I'd like to redecorate it from top to bottom.' That's when I threw my arms around him, and we hugged and hugged. We agreed it would take time, but we had the rest of our lives to see it through.

Mrs Wares had left a lovely supper for us, which we took through to the drawing room, so that when we finished, Rikki could play the piano, which he did quite wonderfully. As he played I gazed around the room. The carpet was white, and two red four-seater sofas faced each other on either side of the fireplace, it felt just like sitting in an old-fashioned railway carriage. The piano, which was black, took up the whole of the bay window and the stark colours of white, red and black made it seem like a stage set. Instead of just going into a room, you felt you had to make an entrance.

When we went up to the bedroom, it too was a nightmare. The furniture was marvellous, but the wallpaper was ghastly, with stripes about two feet apart and the space in-between filled with a floral pattern. And to make matters worse, Ethel had liked it so much that she had bought a second lot to replace the first should it begin to look a bit tired. By now we were the ones who were tired, so we climbed into the comfortable bed, and fell asleep in each other's arms, happily knowing this was only the beginning.

The following morning we had a few hours to ourselves before Mrs Wares came in, and we decided to make breakfast. Rikki had told me what a good chef he was, though my limited experience of his cooking was not encouraging. The only time he invited me to a meal in his Aberdeen house he announced he was going to make his Chicken Mornay Special. This proved to be a tin, courtesy of Crosse & Blackwell, but unfortunately no one had told Rikki that the tin had to be pierced before placing it in boiling water, with the result that the tin angrily exploded with a noise of thunder. I have never seen Chicken Mornay go so far! The floor, the walls, even the windows were covered with the ghastly stuff, and we were grateful to be out of range ourselves.

Remembering this, I suggested that perhaps I could make the bacon and eggs, while he made the coffee. This Rikki readily agreed to, adding that his speciality was frying sausages, which he would do for me one day. Actually he was quite right, I've never known such patience. He would stand by the frying pan for at least half an hour, gently turning them every 30 seconds, until they were just the way he wanted them, jet black and carefully burned. The odd thing was that they tasted rather good!

Before long we were sitting at the kitchen table having our first meal of the day when suddenly we put down our knives and forks at exactly the same moment and started to laugh. What we were laughing at could not be described, it wasn't at anything, or anyone, or at something that had happened – it was just indescribable happiness. We laughed until the tears ran down our faces, at the joy of being together, and so completely and utterly in love.

After we had gathered ourselves, Rikki went to his bathroom for a shower, while I went to the bathroom which was to be mine, and had a bath. This meant that we looked reasonably respectable when Mrs Wares arrived.

The moment Rikki introduced us I realised what a very special person she was, and as we shook hands, I knew that any worries I had imagined were totally unfounded. She was a petite lady with dark hair and the most lovely brown eyes, and the kindest expression – someone you could trust implicitly. She had looked after Rikki ever since he was left on his own, and when she was forced to retire through ill health she told us – we knew that she had two sons of whom she was rightly proud – that she had always looked on Rikki as her third son. No one could have paid him a greater compliment. And how she looked after him! Especially during his 'wild days' when he was on his own and completely free. He told me that it was not unusual for her to come in, in the morning, and find him fast asleep on the bedroom floor. This she solved by getting him into bed, and making a cheese soufflé for his lunch. Her soufflés were out of this world.

The domestic management of the house had a complex history. First of all, Rikki and Ethel had had a housekeeper who lived in, but that had not worked, and it was agreed that she should return to her own family. Then they had a real problem. Both of them were working full time, either in the *Five Past Eight* shows, or in pantomime, and there was no way Ethel could work and run the house at the same time. Then out of the blue came a most unexpected solution. A girl who was in stage management at the King's heard about the situation and announced that she was tired of working in the theatre, and would much rather be their housekeeper. So it was settled, and the girl, Charlotte, a most attractive young woman in her twenties, started work the following week.

I think Rikki and Ethel were most generous when it came to accommodation. Charlotte had a main bedroom at the front of the house with her own bathroom, and also her own sitting room downstairs which had another bathroom off it. It all seemed to work extremely well. However one night when they returned home, Charlotte had a request to make. While she was working in the theatre she had become very friendly with a dancer in the company, the most graceful and beautiful Kay Rose, who had become engaged to Larry Marshall, of 'One O'Clock Gang' fame.

Kay had landed in digs that season which she absolutely hated, so would Rikki and Ethel allow Kay to share Charlotte's room? Since they could see no reason why not, Kay moved in.

There were no problems with the girls, but can you imagine how Rikki felt, as his marriage began to fall apart, knowing that Ethel was having an affair, to be sleeping just through the wall from two very nubile young ladies. Fortunately, beautiful as they were, they didn't appeal to him. Just as well, as it's difficult to imagine Rikki Fulton and Larry Marshall duelling at dawn. Rikki would never have been up in time!

No one expected Kay to do anything in the house, but Rikki found it quite lovable that when Larry's sports car was heard coming round the corner to the house, Kay was always to be found stirring a pot on the stove, presumably something Mrs Wares was preparing for lunch, looking the picture of domesticity. Unfortunately she was a little late getting to the kitchen one time and Larry arrived to find Kay carefully stirring a pot which was full of dish cloths being boiled! I don't think it bothered him one bit, and they have had, and are still having, a wonderfully happy marriage.

9

HOW NOT TO GET A DIVORCE

In 1966, Ethel told Rikki that she was leaving him and going to London. He was amazed, not so much that she was going, but full of admiration at the way she had organised her departure. Trunks and skips had been sent in advance so that on the day she left she probably only needed hand luggage.

There is no way you can escape the pain of parting after years of being together, however wise you both know it is, and Rikki and Ethel both wept very genuine tears as she got into her taxi and disappeared from sight.

Rikki was distraught, and for the first time in his life he was completely alone. He and Ethel had had many problems, but at least she had always been there. Not any more. Not only that, he realised that he hadn't had any food that day, and as there were none of his favourite sausages, he decided he would just have to make do with toast. Having got the bread out, there was an anguished scream from the kitchen – 'the bitch, she's taken the toaster!'

When Ethel left, so did Charlotte. Understandably, to live alone with Rikki would not be a good idea for either of them. Although they liked each other there was no question of romance, and the press might have put their own interpretation on it.

The morning after Ethel left, Rikki had a phone call from Mrs Wares. She had been working as a cleaner under Charlotte, but told Rikki that she had been 'in service' all her life, knew how things should be done and would be very happy to become Rikki's housekeeper.

Suddenly the day seemed brighter – he was going to be looked after, he could get on with his work, and he would no longer have to write Ethel in to every show, as she had demanded.

Not only that, there were all the lovely girls he met in his shows, and on television, and he was a free man! Things were definitely looking up. It was the start of a whole new life!

Many were the flirtations, and brief affairs, one of which was with a girl who was well known. At that time Rikki was doing pantomime in England, and she visited him there at weekends. How the press found out we will never know, but the daily papers had a headline: 'Top Scots Comedian is having an Affair.'

Rikki was furious. There was no way he would ever mention the lady's name, and least of all damage her pristine reputation. He need not have worried. The moment 'Top Scots Comedian' was mentioned, Jimmy Logan called a press conference to vigorously deny he was being unfaithful to his wife, and would sue anyone who dared say so. Rikki slept soundly that night!

Things were not going well for either him, or Jack Milroy, professionally. *Francie and Josie* had had a tremendous success and they had become household names. They say that if parents wanted to get their children in from the back court, all they had to do was open the window and shout 'Francie and Josie are on'. But after some years, Rikki thought the public had probably had enough of them, and took it off television, which did not please Jack.

It's strange to think that the original Francie was, in fact, Stanley Baxter, in a sketch in the *Five Past Eight Show*, but it never got off the ground. Rikki and he could never have worked together – they were not on the same wavelength.

Some time later Rikki saw Jack Milroy at the Ayr Gaiety Theatre, and thought he was brilliant, so he asked Jack if he would like to play Francie, and that was the start of a wonderful relationship, both on and off stage. The difference between working with Stanley Baxter and Jack was quite obvious to an audience. Baxter is rightly admired, but he is a solo star, not one of a partnership, whereas Rikki and Jack seemed to create a chemistry which was magical. They just loved working together, and people enjoyed seeing that.

When the series ended, STV gave Rikki and Jack a series each. I believe Jack's wasn't good, but Rikki's was an unmitigated disaster. He maintained that the director, Bryan Izzard, very nearly put him out of the business. Rikki said that the scripts were dreadful as was the direction and after a short time he refused to do any more, so I think doing a season in Aberdeen was something of an escape – only that wasn't going well either! I've always been rather glad that I met Rikki at the nadir of his career – no one could accuse me of wanting him for his stardom!

We came back to Glasgow in 1967 and shortly afterwards Rikki was in a show at the Alhambra, and the other comedian was Norman Vaughan. The two of them got along tremendously well, unless they were playing table tennis. Rikki had developed quite a talent for it, and he always won, although Norman was quick to point out that he was playing at a great disadvantage. When he played at home in Croydon his manager was always there to pick up the balls, and in Glasgow he had to pick them up for himself.

Norman came to stay with us, and I couldn't have been more pleased, because I had been offered an announcing contract with Tyne Tees Television and when I was away Rikki wouldn't be alone.

It was rather an unusual contract. Tyne Tees only employed female announcers and we would each work for two and a half days and then be free for the rest of the week. I used to drive down at dawn on a Sunday, open the station, and work all day and night, the same on Monday, and I would be free by Tuesday lunchtime to drive home to the love of my life!

It was a marvellous feeling to open the front door and hear gales of laughter coming from whatever room Rikki and Norman were in. We were all having a lovely time together, the panto-mime was going very well, and when the men came home from work all I had to do was heat the supper Mrs Wares had left for us, and pour the drinks. It was hardly slave labour, and Rikki and I were rather enjoying being host and hostess for the first time.

We had many pleasant weeks, and then Rikki told me that Norman's wife was coming up to join us. 'That's lovely,' I said. 'Much nicer to have a foursome, and to have two women looking after you.'

How wrong can you be? She, her name was Bernice, arrived when I was working at Tyne Tees, so that by the time I got back she was already established. I told her how glad I was that she had come, because now Norman's happiness would be complete, but even as I spoke I could feel my voice trailing away. The look on her face said it all. I even began to think wistfully about Irene Handl – by comparison she had looked like a Fairy Godmother.

Bernice had decided to treat me as the hired help, and would tell me that she would like a cup of coffee, to which I would give her a very sweet smile and say, 'What a good idea, Bernice, I think you know where the kitchen is. You'll find it all laid out.'

From then on it was war. She complained about the guest room they were in and would much prefer one of the others. I was very glad that Rikki ignored the complaint. But Bernice seemed to have a plan to get rid of me. Rikki's reputation with the ladies during his spell of freedom was well known, and there was a girl in the pantomime that she was sure would usurp me. Joanna was a lovely girl, both in looks and in her nature.

Bernice and Norman always invited Rikki out for supper after the show on a Monday, and of course Joanna would be asked to make up the foursome. I always phoned Rikki last thing at night, and one Monday when we talked he could hardly put two words together, and his voice would disappear completely. This worried me because it was always a sign that he was in a bad depression. The next day, instead of going to Glasgow I had to go to Aberdeen to Grampian TV, and wouldn't be back with Rikki until about two or three in the morning. So I decided that instead of driving up the east coast from Newcastle to Aberdeen, I could go to Glasgow for half an hour to see how he was.

On my journey north I passed a florist with some beautiful flowers in the window, and I thought that might just cheer Rikki up. So armed with the flowers in a lovely bouquet I arrived at the house. Before I could use my key Mrs Wares opened the door: 'Oh Kate, I'm so glad you've come, I just don't know what to do; he's been miserable ever since you left.'

I asked her where he was and she told me he was in the drawing room with *them*. Giving her the flowers, I went in to see the man I loved. He was sitting alone and looking very disconsolate, while the rest of the room was taken up by Norman, Bernice and Joanna. Rikki took me in his arms and said he didn't think he was going to see me today. I told him it was only for a few minutes, but I had been worried about him after our phone call, it was depression wasn't it? He started to say 'Yes, it was,' when Bernice interrupted with, 'You never have to worry about him when we're here, and particularly when Joanna is here too.' At that point Mrs Wares came in with a large vase containing the flowers I had brought and as she passed Rikki she said loudly, 'That girl is a gem,' nodding in my direction, and as she placed the vase right in front of Bernice, said even more loudly 'a gem'.

I had never seen her as irate before, but when Bernice told me with a slight smile that Joanna had stayed the night, I understood why Mrs Wares had been so angry. Bernice had made sure that Mrs Wares always knew where Rikki and Joanna were, especially when she and Norman had tactfully left 'the lovely couple' alone together.

Sadly for Bernice, and thankfully for me, her romantic plot didn't work. Rikki liked Joanna very much, he enjoyed working with her and loved her singing voice. She enjoyed his company, and loved his piano playing, but that was all they had in common. What Rikki and I were sorry about was the change that came over Norman. From the moment his wife arrived it was as though he had all the fun drained out of him, and he actually became tetchy. No longer were there the late-night laughter sessions, instead he would get cross if Rikki or I wanted to use our cars, because to get them out of the garage and onto the road meant Norman having to move his Jaguar from the driveway.

The day they left I said goodbye to Norman on his own, and got into my car, but not quite quickly enough. As I began to reverse down our drive there was a loud knocking on the window. Of course it was Bernice. I had decided not to bid farewell to her, just disappear, but she was determined to have the last word. I opened the window and she thrust her head into the car saying, 'All I can say to you Kate is "Good Luck", you're certainly going to need it.' I didn't reply, just pressed a button and the window closed just missing her hastily withdrawn nose. I continued down the drive, but gave her a very happy wave as I turned into the road. It was the least I could do for a departing guest!

After our guests had left, it was so good to enjoy just being together again, and Mrs Wares was much happier too! Now that we were settled, and ecstatically happy, it seemed natural for me to get to know Rikki's friends in Glasgow, and what a lot there were. The first two had been his friends from schooldays and through the war. Gordon had been in the Air Force, Margo in the ATS, and Rikki in the Navy, but somehow they always managed to arrange their leave at the same time.

When Gordon and Margo married, and Rikki married Ethel, it looked as though it would make a nice foursome, but Ethel didn't want to know. So it was only after she had left that the

'Terrible Trio' met up again, and what a reunion that was!

Rikki had been seeing them regularly when he was on his own and they were most welcoming to me. I liked them both very much indeed and we spent many happy years in their company.

One friend to whom I needed no introduction was Clem Ashby, who had been working with Rikki for years with Howard and Wyndham, but he still loved to reminisce about the Perth Theatre days. There were two other friends whom I didn't know, one was the very successful businessman, Sir Iain Stewart, and the other was Sean Connery. The four of them were all keen golfers and decided to call themselves the WIF Club. The abbreviation standing for 'Women Is Funny'. Perhaps the fact that all four of them were divorced tended to colour their judgement. They had all had quite enough of wives and solemnly swore never to marry again. Eventually three of them did, so I suppose that as the only remaining bachelor, Clem won that round.

The first time I met Sean was at Iain's for dinner, and at that time he was still married to the beautiful Diane Cilento. I will never forget meeting her. She was stunning, not only in looks but she was also witty, most interesting to listen to with that beautiful voice, and above all she conveyed a genuine feeling of warmth towards the people around her, and those she talked about. Rikki and I were saddened by the marriage break-up.

I now was facing a much closer break-up of my own, that of Graham and myself. I found it most difficult to tell him that there could be no going back. He had been supremely kind in every way, and I could never thank him enough for rescuing me from London. He was and is a remarkable man. The one thing at the back of my mind was the fact that on two or three occasions when I had phoned him in Aberdeen, and he was out working, a girl had answered. The second time it happened I told her my name and asked for hers, but all she would say was that she was a friend of Graham's. It would beggar belief if we had both found the person we wanted to marry at exactly the same time.

But we had! Graham and Ann wanted to be together as much as Rikki and I did. It was just too good to be true.

The big drawback was the divorce proceedings, which took so long. England had introduced a much more civilised system, which only called for a breakdown of the marriage, but in Scotland there still had to be the guilty and the innocent party, which had to be proved. It had been hoped that the 'breakdown' clause would apply to Scotland as well, but it was halted by Glasgow MP Tom Galbraith, who caused misery to families for years, while he himself got his own divorce in England under their laws.

In Rikki's case, Ethel would be divorcing him, and this she did with great consideration; she wasn't going to name me so we had to dream up a situation that would satisfy the divorce court.

Rikki, being a most law-abiding citizen, decided the only thing to do was to consult his lawyer. This he did and the dear man was only too helpful with his advice. First of all, we had to be discovered in a compromising situation (we took that to mean in bed together), and preferably not in Glasgow, but over on the East coast – I suppose to make it look like a weekend, playing away from home. Then Rikki asked our lawyer the crucial question, 'Where do you suggest we should book a room?' The very distinguished gentleman thought for some time, and then said, 'I am told that The Open Arms in Dirleton is excellent,' and this without the flicker of a smile!

The following week we dutifully set off, rather looking forward to our illicit rendezvous. We enjoyed the drive so much. It was winter, very cold and clear, and we were beginning to start the necessary divorces which would give us both our freedom. Rikki loved driving, and we both enjoyed the warmth of the car and listening to Frank Sinatra. I couldn't help thinking how fortunate we were that the two couples involved both very much wanted these divorces. No one was going to be left on their own, and thankfully there were no children involved.

We arrived at the Open Arms and found them as suggested by their name, most welcoming. We went over to reception through a lovely entrance hall with a most inviting coal fire, large comfortable armchairs, and small tables filled with newspapers and magazines. Having carefully signed in as Mr and Mrs, we followed our cases to our room. Rikki was quite tired from all the driving, so that when I suggested that while I dressed for dinner he should go down and enjoy a relaxing drink in one of those armchairs, he was only too happy to agree, and we said we would meet at 7.30. I had a shower and dressed, and made sure that I was going to be down in time, because Rikki was a firm believer in punctuality.

Arriving on the dot I expected at least a welcoming kiss. There was none. In fact there was no one! Rikki had disappeared. My only reaction was how dare someone stand you up when you are there to help them get a divorce? Within two minutes the front door opened, and Rikki stood there convulsed in laughter. He explained that he had been reading the paper in the chair with its back to the door, when two men dressed in raincoats with hats straight out of a 1950s film stood behind him and asked: 'Are you Rikki Fulton?' When he admitted that was the case, they insisted that he should follow them outside. Thinking this was some kind of a joke he went along with it, only to find that they were the private detectives who were to discover us in the morning giving Ethel grounds for divorce.

When they left we ordered two drinks, and drank a toast to Ethel and Graham. If only they knew what we were going through for their sakes! After a most enjoyable meal, we went back to our room, and for the first time registered the fact that the room had twin beds. Nonetheless we decided that having got so far, we would not give in, and decided that when the men came in the morning, they would discover us both in the same bed.

The next day I got up at 7.30. It is one thing to be caught 'in flagrante' but quite another to be caught with dishevelled hair and no make-up. We climbed into one bed, naked as usual, and waited for a knock on the door. We were both getting giggly about the whole absurd nonsense we had been forced into, and had to restrain ourselves from enjoying it too much. At eight thirty instead of a knock at the door, the phone rang. It was the girl at the reception desk, apologising very much for disturbing us so early, but there were two men asking for Mr Fulton. Should she say he was not available and send them packing?

Rikki thanked her for her concern but said he had been expecting the gentlemen, to discuss a business contract, and would she please send them to our room. Moments later the private detectives appeared, still in the raincoats but now carrying clipboards. They said they would like to ask Rikki some questions if he was agreeable, which of course he was. Needing to have no part in the ensuing conversation, I just nestled back in Rikki's arms and listened to them. It all seemed pretty straightforward, answering questions about the life he and Ethel had shared, and Rikki took all the blame for the break-up of their marriage.

I really had to bite my tongue hard at that; it was so unfair. Their relationship had been over for some time, so why were we having to lie and go through this charade to have it ended? Then I realised they were all looking at me, and the question-master asked Rikki, 'What is her name?' Rikki's eyes became icy cold, and he told them there was no way he was going to give it to them. They stood up and told us there was no point in going on and the whole thing had been a waste of time. When we asked why, they told us that they had been told it was going to be a one-night stand, and men don't mind giving the woman's name; that's what she is being paid for.

In a kind of desperation I asked them that if all our efforts had been in vain, what should we have done? The Private Eyes by now had become much more friendly, as though they were no longer on duty, which I don't suppose they were, and said if it could be proved that we were living together that would be enough. 'What proof would you need?' I asked.

'Do you have any clothes at Mr Fulton's home?'

At this point, Rikki who had been having a glass of water choked and sprayed it all over the room. I suppose because the bedroom he had given me to keep my clothes in was so full it was difficult to shut the door! In answer to the question, I replied, 'Just a few,' and they said, 'That's all we would have needed.' So all was not lost.

They were to come to the house that evening to find the glaring evidence.

When they left, we both felt the same. We had started out on a champagne night which would bring us closer to being together, but now all we felt was grubby, and the whole episode seemed sordid. We both felt very much in need of a shower, and having had them, we dressed and went straight to the car. We were in no mood for breakfast.

We held each other very close before we got into the car, because we knew we were each feeling exactly the same – but it was too soon to talk about it. Rikki drove for about three miles then pulled the Mercedes over. And all he said was, 'Would you like to drive?'

We changed seats, and I was at the wheel of Rikki's beautiful car. It was a dream to drive, and I kept driving until we arrived at what I was beginning to think of as 'home'. True to their word our private detectives arrived at the house at about 7pm. They were much more friendly than they had been in Dirleton, and seemed to be quite enjoying themselves. We poured them drinks, and chatted for a while, and then I took them upstairs to see the incriminating evidence. They tried without success to hide their smiles when they saw my 'just a few' clothes bursting out of the wardrobes, but then when they went into the master bedroom and found my dressing gown lying beside Rikki's on the bed, they said they now had sufficient evidence to prove Rikki's adultery. What an ugly word. We preferred to think that without harming anyone at all, we were so in love, and blissfully happy.

By now we were into winter and I had left Tyne Tees TV. Rikki was under contract to do pantomime in Oxford with Bruce Forsyth and no way could we be apart for weeks. Clem, of course, would be working with Rikki, and that raised a bit of a problem. Up until now whenever they were working away from home the two of them always shared a house or a flat, and Rikki was in a quandary about what to do this time. I tried to tell him not to worry – if Clem wanted to share then of course he should do so, as long as he accepted that we would be a threesome, but certainly not a *ménage à trois*.

10

THE DOG WATCH

Some time before we went south Rikki and I made a commitment to each other which was in every way as important as a marriage certificate, and meant that whatever happened we had to stay together. We bought two West Highland puppies! We had been told of an excellent breeder of Westies, and she had a new litter for sale. To dog lovers like us, it was irresistible. We drove over to see them and they were breathtakingly lovely. We wanted two so they would be company for each other. We chose one of the best-looking and friendly dogs, and then we asked which was the runt of the litter. He was certainly smaller than the others, but that seemed the only difference and we just felt that he of all of them should have a big brother to look after him.

The extrovert we called Jonathon, and the introvert, because he seemed to be a more serious little dog, and anxious to please, we called Jeeves. Now we felt really established. No way could we ever separate – who would get custody of the dogs?

We did as we would always do when getting dogs. Rikki would drive, and I would hold the puppies in a sheepskin coat on my lap. I've always felt rather strongly about that, because when you take a tiny puppy from its siblings and from its home, wrapping it into a warm sheepskin and holding it close must be very comforting. They always slept all the way home, but there was no doubt that they bonded with whoever was holding them and Rikki missed out on those moments. But it didn't take them long to discover who was the master of the household and behave accordingly!

The thought of taking them to Oxford was daunting. They were only eight weeks old, but somehow or other we were going to get there. Rikki drove, Clem had the whole back seat to himself, and I sat beside Rikki, with the comforting sheepskin and two puppies on my lap.

We couldn't believe how peacefully it all worked out. The pups were fed and watered regularly and grumbled when they were put on the grass at the service stations, but apart from that they just slept. Rikki and Clem, however, managed to have a couple of meals at the stations, and were magnanimous enough to bring me sandwiches!

The Oxford Theatre had been kind enough to arrange a flat for the three of us, on the outskirts of Oxford in a delightful village called Eynsham. We found the flat quite easily, though we were a little surprised to find it was over a grocery store, rather like a Spar shop. I liked the idea very much, visualising asking Clem if he would like tomato sauce with his sausage, bacon and egg, and if he did, saying, 'give me two minutes', rushing downstairs, buying it and being back before the bacon had got cold. I could see great potential in our winter home.

It was when we went to bed that we discovered the snag in the flat. We were extremely tired after the long journey, and having settled the pups in their beds, we were only too happy to turn out the light. Then the noise started. There was an attic above us, and the noise was deafening. We couldn't think what it was but it seemed to be orchestrated. We then agreed that it must be mice in the attic, but if it was, they must have been enormous, and definitely wearing clogs!

The next morning we told our landlord about it and he wasn't at all surprised. 'We have always had this problem, being over a food shop,' he said, 'but don't you worry, by the time you get home tonight there won't be a mouse to be heard.' He was right – there was total silence from the attic. Instead Rikki and I lay in our bed, hand in hand, feeling awful that we had caused the deaths of so many mice. I'm sure we could have learned to enjoy their clog dance.

The following day was the start of the rehearsals, and after a hearty breakfast, on Clem's part but not on Rikki's, they drove to the theatre. I knew Rikki was looking forward to working with Bruce Forsyth – he had a great admiration for his many talents and liked him.

Strangely enough, Rikki could have had a similar career to Bruce's. He had gained a good reputation in presenting the Showband Show, and also as a compère of all the orchestras in the Royal Albert Hall. He had come to the notice of a man I can only think of as the 'Godfather'. His name was Billy Marsh, and he had theatre and television in London sewn up. If you were with Billy Marsh you were home and dry. Bruce had been presenting *Sunday Night at the London Palladium* for some weeks, and needed a break, a holiday, and Billy Marsh decided that Rikki Fulton was the man to take over. You can imagine how Rikki felt – this really was the big time. He worked flat out on a script as he was expected to provide comedy throughout the evening and introduce the guest artists.

In those days all the television programmes were live and that's where the trouble lay! Rikki welcomed the viewers, and used a small part of his script, then introduced the first act. He waited in the wings for his next spot before he introduced the second act. Suddenly the stage manager was at his side, looking extremely worried and sweating profusely, 'Rikki, cut your spot, they've over-run,' and that was the format for the night. Rikki went on dutifully to introduce the acts and that was all he could do. All the comedy he had worked so hard to prepare was lost (though knowing Rikki, I bet it turned up elsewhere!).

At the end of the performance Billy Marsh himself came backstage and said to Rikki, 'Congratulations Rikki, wonderful show, no problems, and you got us down in time. Now about you taking over *Sunday Night at the London Palladium* next week.' At which point Rikki said, very calmly, 'Mr Marsh, you can take your *Sunday Night at the London Palladium*, and shove it up your f****** arse.'

And with that Rikki returned to Scotland.

I am so very glad that he did. I don't think the work he would have been doing in London could ever have been as fulfilling as the work he did in Scotland. I am sure he would never have been short of work and would have made a great deal more money, but that could never have made up for the joy he had playing to his own folk, and the tremendous range of parts he was allowed to enjoy, from Francie and Josie to Shakespeare, from Scotch and Wry to Molière. Scotland really gave him his freedom, and he loved it. David Jacobs took over from Rikki when he left the Showband Show and made a very successful career of presenting. It was right for him, but it could never have been right for Rikki.

For now though, it was Oxford and pantomime, but not really as we know it north of the border – they are quite different in England. For the Scots the comedy is all important but down south the costumes and most particularly the guest star take precedence, and though I have to admit I am most certainly biased, pantomimes never seem to have as much warmth and sheer fun as they do in Scotland.

Bruce Forsyth was one of the biggest names in show business at that time, and the company were expecting the House Full board to be seen daily. It never happened. No one could under-stand it, and I still don't. One theory was that Bruce had perhaps been on television too much, so why would people pay money to come out on a cold winter's night to watch him in pantomime. Whatever the reason, it affected Bruce badly in terms of his health and he was frequently unwell. Guess who they asked to take over from him when he was off? The one and only Norman Vaughan! Thankfully Bernice did not accompany him, so we were allowed to enjoy ourselves in Oxford.

We were paid a surprise visit by Sir Iain and Sean Connery who came unannounced to the pantomime, and we all went out for a very pleasant meal afterwards, to one of the eating places we liked in Oxford. As we were finishing our meal I was regaled with the story of the three of them and Glen Michael on a golfing afternoon in Ayrshire. One of Sean's James Bond films had just been released, and Sean could get no peace at all from the press and fans. He was desperate to go somewhere nobody knew him, and Glen very kindly suggested that he with Iain and Rikki should spend the day at his home in Ayrshire. There Sean could relax completely and enjoy his wife Beryl's excellent home cooking, and then they could have a foursome for golf in the afternoon. Glen Michael is perhaps best remembered from his long running children's series *Cartoon Cavalcade*, but before that he was Jack Milroy's 'feed' in *Five Past Eight* and in Francie and Josie, and a nicer and warmer couple than Glen and Beryl would be hard to find. After a delicious lunch, which Sean particularly enjoyed – it made such a change from hotel food – the four men headed for the golf club.

I gather that by this time Glen was wondering if this was a good idea after all! What he had forgotten was just what he was up against. Iain was President of the Royal and Ancient Golf Club in St Andrews, Sean was known worldwide as an excellent golfer, and Rikki at that time was crazy about the game and played every day. It was decided that Glen should start the proceedings, so shaking with nerves he drove off. Unfortunately his ball didn't even venture towards the first hole but sliced sharply to the right, cleared a very high hedge and landed neatly in a freight wagon on a train going to Aberdeen.

There was dead silence, broken only by Rikki who remarked

with an absolutely straight face, 'Well, that must be the longest drive of the day.'

The rest of our time in Oxford passed pleasantly, and I had time to look after the puppies. They were adorable and after they had their jags from the vet I could take them out for walks, which at first they hated! Collars and leads were not appreciated, but after a few days they decided walks were fun and became quite adventurous.

The nearer it got to Christmas the more I realised just what a delightful village we were in. The people were very friendly, and walking the dogs through snow to the butcher to order the turkey, I felt I was treading in generations of footprints.

I bought an artificial white Christmas tree and spent some time decorating it. What a waste of time! The gentlemen with whom I lived couldn't have cared less. That was understandable – on stage they were surrounded by tinsel and glitter and really only wanted to get a rest from it all when they came home. But they managed very fixed grins of delight when they saw the tree, and I realised I had a lot to learn about making performers happy and relaxed when they came home.

The dogs were wonderful, they were now completely house-trained, and Jeeves never put a paw wrong. Jonathon was a different story. I had worried about him since we were on a country lane one day and I had let them off their leads when he saw cows for the first time in his life. He looked at them very carefully, and then told Jeeves who was muttering that they looked dangerous, 'Nonsense, they're just big dogs,' and headed into the field to play with them. Fortunately the cows didn't seem to mind him being there, but when he started sniffing at their hooves, and licking their noses when they were grazing, enough was enough. The herd chased him for his life, and you've never seen a Westie move so fast. He hurtled through the fence and begged to have his lead put back on.

That wasn't our only problem with Jonathon. We had made a

bed for the dogs in the kitchen, which they seemed happy with. There was no sound during the night from them, except for the odd crunching noise, which we couldn't account for, but all seemed well.

When we tidied up the flat at the end of our stay in Oxford we discovered what the crunching noise had been. Underneath the kitchen table Jonathon had painstakingly eaten through the wall! There was a large hole which displayed the cavity wall, and if he had had another week he would have eaten himself into the hall! Not only that, but the linoleum around his handy work had also been removed. Presumably chewed and swallowed.

It was then that I learned what a talent Rikki had for DIY. I don't know what he used, but it looked as though the wall had never had a hole in it. The linoleum was much more of a problem – that couldn't be faked. Eventually, we moved a cabinet that sat firmly on the ground, and removed the linoleum underneath it, when we put it back it looked the same as it had always done, but now Rikki had enough pieces to make a very successful jigsaw puzzle on the floor, and the kitchen looked just as it did when we arrived.

I was a little worried about what the pups would be like on our journey home. They were quite a bit bigger than they had been on the journey south, but they were still small enough to curl up on my knee in their sheepskin, and they couldn't have behaved better.

There was one incident on the road I will never forget. We were on a dual carriageway an hour out of Oxford, and every-thing was going smoothly. The road was busy, but being a Sunday not nearly as busy as a weekday. Suddenly an Austin Mini appeared on the inside lane, driving far too fast for a small car, and cut in front of us with no indication whatsoever. Rikki had to do emergency braking, and blasted the horn. It had no effect at all, and moments later the Mini was off again cutting in on another car, and another, and another – by which time everyone on the road was fascinated by this appalling driving (I may say it was a man at the wheel, not a woman driver!). Then the road went into a long bend, and the Mini was out of sight. There were several small grassy hillocks along the route as roundabouts, and as we came round the bend we could see one ahead, only this one was different from all the others. It had a small Austin Mini firmly wedged on the top of it! Obviously the idiot driver had taken the bend far too fast, and had gone right up the grass of the roundabout where he was now completely stuck. You can imagine the reaction of all the cars to which he had given trouble. There wasn't one who didn't blow their horn, or cheer, or make an unmistakable gesture . . .

Clem was very quiet on the journey home. I think his worst fears were now confirmed. Rikki told me years later that Clem did everything in his power to stop Rikki from marrying me, and I'm not at all surprised. It meant the end of the two of them sharing a flat when they worked out of Glasgow, something which I know Clem very much enjoyed, as he did having company for a meal out after the show, and then being driven home. In fact Clem and I got along together very well, and I was an avid admirer of his talent for crosswords. He and the witty Cliff Hanley were masters of the game, and each year they would be finalists in the London *Times* competition, a famously difficult one to solve. From now on Clem would have to be much more self-sufficient and that wasn't something to which he looked forward.

Rikki as always was overjoyed to be home. I was too, and the dogs were positively ecstatic. Now they had the complete freedom of the back garden, which we had thought was safely enclosed, but needless to say Jonathon managed to dig a tunnel under the trellis fence and was just small enough to squeeze through the metal fence on the other side, and he insisted that Jeeves go with him. When we realised they'd gone we had to go round the block to our neighbouring drive to get them back, but they were growing so fast that within a fortnight they were too big to get through the fence and we could all relax.

We enjoyed a few weeks of peace and quiet. Rikki did some television for Granada, and I was working for Border Television, but the one company I really wanted to work for was STV. Unfortunately they had stopped employing female announcers. They had had a problem with an actress who had no experience of announcing, so I don't think she could be blamed. After all they had offered her the job, but it was mutually agreed that her contract should be terminated, and the powers that be said no more women announcers.

This was now 1968, and a whole new situation had arrived for television. It was the year of the Mexico Olympics, and for the first time television was to be on air from 7am till 3am. The trouble was there weren't enough announcers to go round!

Having looked through their files for anyone who had applied to them, STV wrote to ask if I would like to work for them. Wouldn't I just! There was a problem though: I was under contract to Border for the Olympics, so I told STV that if I sent them my schedule for Border and they could fit theirs to it, I would be delighted to join them, and that's what they did.

Rikki couldn't understand why I was so tremendously happy about it, but when I explained that if I worked efficiently, perhaps they would employ me again, he understood. The thought of being able to work from home, and never having to leave Rikki again, was paramount in my mind.

What I hadn't bargained for was the time schedule. On paper it looked fine, but when I started working it I realised that the one thing that I hadn't allowed for was sleep! In the morning I would open the Glasgow station at 7am, and when I left in the evening I would drive to Carlisle to open Border TV at 7am and the following day I would do the evening shift, ending at 3am and then driving back to Glasgow to open the station at 7am. By the end of three weeks I was a walking zombie. But it was worth every minute of it, because at the end of it I was offered a contract by STV.

I stayed with them for thirteen very happy years. Rikki and I could hardly believe our luck, and to add to our happiness, if that is the right word, Rikki's divorce from Ethel came through. She had been so very kind, Rikki was divorced for adultery, but she didn't name me, as she had every right to do. The press were also wonderful – they could have had a field day but the divorce was mentioned in a few lines well inside the paper and that was it over.

I was concerned that however calm Rikki had seemed when Ethel left, the finality of divorce might really hit him, but it didn't. They were two highly intelligent people who had realised they no longer wanted to be together, and the farce that had to be gone through to achieve their freedom seemed ludicrous, but then that was 1968!

11

PARADISE IN POLLENSA

After all the turmoil of the past few months Rikki thought it was time we had a holiday, and by sheer chance he was asked to make a commercial for a travel company. Wisely, instead of a fee he asked for a fortnight's holiday for two in their best hotel, and we went to lovely Puerto Pollensa, in the north of Majorca. In a way this too was a testing time – were we compatible on holiday? Thankfully we seemed to be, and enjoyed every minute. The only problem was that Rikki didn't like sitting in the sun but I did. We solved that by Rikki staying in our suite, while I sat out on the balcony, but we could talk to each other and with a bit of a stretch hold hands! It really was the first time we had been completely on our own, and neither of us could believe how incredibly wonderful it was. I was still afraid that I was going to wake up. How could I be allowed to spend 24 hours a day with the man who meant more to me than life itself, and be told he was enjoying it as much as I was!

It wasn't long before we found the zenith of relaxation. There were a number of small boats in the bay which never seemed to be sailed, so we bought two inflatable lilos and swam with them out to the boats; there we wound the mooring ropes around our wrists and floated on the lilos for the whole afternoon. Under these circumstances Rikki didn't mind being in the sun at all, the lilos stayed cool while we enjoyed the sun, and the gentle movement of the sea soon had us dozing in heavenly, happy peace. Whenever I become angry or fraught I try very hard to remember what those afternoons of total relaxation were like. Occasionally it works!

We came home to something that had never been tried before. Jimmy Logan had bought the theatre at St George's Cross, which was now called Jimmy Logan's Metropole, and he wanted to do a play with Francie and Josie. I'm not sure who wrote it, but it seemed to be very successful, the audiences liked it, the management liked it, Rikki liked it, and Jack hated it! I don't think he had been in a play before. Usually he was doing Variety, where he would do his spot in the first act, go to his dressing room and relax before his spot in the second act, then the finale and home. He couldn't believe that for a play he had to stay in the wings for the whole night, waiting for a cue, going on to do just one scene, then coming off to wait in the wings once more until the next scene. It just wasn't show business as Jack knew it, and the sooner it was over, the better.

I only saw the production on the last night because I was under contract to Ulster TV for three weeks, and as Rikki was busy in the theatre it seemed like a good time to go. I didn't want to work away from home, but I really was glad that I had gone. I liked the Irish people so much, they were always friendly, and their sense of humour was just like Glaswegian's. Admittedly you had to have a sense of fun to work in their television station!

On my second morning there I was surprised to hear the opening music, it seemed to be rather early, but I thought the studio clock was probably wrong, it usually was. As the music began to fade away I got an urgent call from Transmission Control, 'Kate, you'll have to fill for five minutes.' Before I had a chance to ask anyone what was going on I saw in the monitor that the camera was on and I was on all the screens in Ulster. Five minutes doesn't sound very long, does it? But I can assure you, when you don't have the faintest idea what to talk about, it can seem like a lifetime! All I could do was grab the TV Times and tell the viewers what the morning's programmes would be. Hardly imaginative!

Then I couldn't believe my luck. One of the first programmes was *Mr Ed*. It was American, and I'm not sure anyone remembers it, but it was about a beautiful Palomino horse who could talk, had a far greater intelligence than humans and always got the better of them.

Some time back I had bought a two-year-old filly and with the help of my friend Biddy I broke her in. Biddy just happened to have a Palomino stud farm, and as I was there every day I learned quite a bit about them. Therefore the Irish viewers, enjoying their breakfast, were no doubt puzzled by this strange woman who kept talking about horses, for no apparent reason.

When at last the wretched five minutes were over, and we were back on the scheduled programme, I dared to ask what the problem had been. I got a perfectly reasonable explanation, 'Billy [the controller] misread the time so we were on the air five minutes early.' There was no answer to that, was there?

My other favourite moment at Ulster was the short bit of religion before close down. What was laughingly called the announcer's studio, was more like a coffin than anything else. It was extremely narrow, with one small desk, one chair, one microphone and one camera. Quite adequate for one person, but try getting two in there!

Yet that is what we had to do when we came to the close down. The cleric, of whatever denomination, naturally had to be in the chair for the camera, for the equivalent of STV's Late Call. The problem was that I had to use the microphone before him for a voice-over announcement. There was only one solution: I would have to sit on his knee while I read the Greyhound Racing results, and then sit at his feet, out of view, while it was his turn. The clergyman of the week turned out to be a wonderful rotund Catholic, who thought it would be much better if we were both on camera, and he would prophesy the Greyhound results before I read them out! I could only thank my lucky stars that I was paired with a portly Priest, and not an angular Anglican – the Priest's lap was extremely comfortable!

It was so marvellous to be back with Rikki that I vowed never to work away from home again, and I never did.

Now that the comedy at the Metropole was over, another one started in real life. Jack had been asked to do the Pavilion pantomime, which was great for him, but he and Rikki were so used to working together that he asked Rikki if he would join him, and they could do a Francie and Josie pantomime. That seemed like an excellent idea and Rikki was only too happy to agree. Unfortunately the man putting on the show did not. He was Eric Popplewell, who ran Ayr Gaiety Theatre, and he was adamant that it was not going to be a Francie and Josie pantomime, it was going to be Jack on his own. Perhaps he felt that Francie and Josie had had their day, and it would be a mistake to revive them.

Meanwhile, back at the drawing board, Rikki and Jack were working on a cabaret act which they were to do at the Edinburgh Festival in the Palladium Theatre. Ross Bowie had been their agent for some time, and had booked them into many of the Clyde resorts, which gave me an idea. One day I suggested to Rikki that it might be a good idea to try out their new material somewhere like Largs.

'Whatever for?' he asked.

'It would give you confidence for the Festival, and if it's successful, word might get back to Eric Popplewell.'

They only did three nights at Largs. The first night, a Thursday, they had a full house, the following night they were having to turn people away, and on the Saturday, tickets could be bought on the black market!

The following week Eric Popplewell decided a Francie and Josie pantomime would be a very good idea. Both Rikki and Jack sighed, 'If only *we* had thought of that!'

1969 was turning out to be a very eventful year. Graham had divorced me in January, and although both Rikki and I were named, once again the papers were very kind to us, and really only mentioned the fact without writing an article about it.

Freedom for us both came as a bit of a shock, and we soon realised that we liked the situation very much, and neither of us wanted to change it in any way. That may have suited Rikki and me, but it certainly didn't please my father. He assumed that the moment we were both free, we would marry at once, and when we didn't he really began to worry. He had hoped our holiday in Pollensa would be our honeymoon, and even wrote Rikki a nice letter to the effect that he would be welcomed as one of the family. To this Rikki replied in the most polite way, and explained that we just wanted time to recover from the trauma of divorce and enjoy a really peaceful time in the company of each other. This did nothing to placate Daddy.

He stormed at my mother, 'You see. They're not even going to get married. Well, I won't set foot in their house until they do.' And he never did.

Mummy on the other hand was a frequent visitor, very often with a bridge friend for afternoon tea, and I think it was then that she and Rikki realised how very much they liked each other, and that never changed. In the summer the two of them would sit in the garden for hours just talking. They would discuss their respective childhoods, the war, the many changes in Glasgow, their parents, their dogs, and never once did they run out of conversation. I think too that Rikki found Mummy relaxing to be with. He had told me that his first mother-in-law used to annoy him by gathering all the dishes as they were used during a meal, and take them through to wash them in the kitchen before the next course could be served, leaving his housekeeper with nothing to do. Mummy showed not the slightest inclination to go anywhere near the kitchen, and that's how Rikki liked it. She also had a tremendous capacity for laughing at herself, which is always lovable.

Before I left Tyne Tees TV Rikki had a birthday, and I decided to give him a surprise party, just a small dinner party, but I was soon in trouble with guests. I invited Gordon and Margo, a friend of Rikki's and a champion table tennis player whom Rikki loved to play, and beat. Dick was his name, he was a doctor, and was charming as well as being tall, dark and handsome. Clem of course would be there, and I also invited Iain, who said that Sean would be staying with him that night, and of course he also was welcome to join us.

All the guests were marvellous and didn't say a word to Rikki about their invitations, so he had no idea what was going on. He didn't even catch Mrs Wares and me hiding avocados and melons on window ledges to ripen. The problem was that we had too many men. There were six of them and only Margo and myself.

I really had to have at least one other woman, but at that time I didn't know any in Glasgow. Then I thought of a fellow announcer at Tyne Tees. She was a most attractive young woman, whose name was Ruth. She had long blonde hair and a figure that would have swept the board in a Miss World contest and she was also good fun. It had seemed to me that her only problem was her hands. This was the time of the mini skirt, and Ruth's could not have been more mini without being arrested, and the cleavage of her shirts went right down to her waist. And for some reason she was completely butter fingered. I can't remember a meal in the canteen when she didn't drop something, and as she bent down to retrieve it all the men in the room would stand up, as though to help her, but Ruth was much too independent for that, and giving them all a lovely smile, she would return to her table. The men then sat down, although I couldn't help noticing that some seemed rather uncomfortable.

Ruth was very popular. We each had flatlets in the same house, and although we were friendly I didn't see much of her, as she was out a great deal, and I was only there for Sunday and Monday nights. When I asked her if she would like to come to Rikki's party, and stay the night with us, she was most enthusiastic about the idea. I was so glad I had asked her, and was sure she would be good company.

Rikki had been told that I was preparing a romantic birthday dinner for the two of us, but he wasn't allowed to go into the dining room until I served the meal. He made no objections whatsoever, just poured us drinks, and we sat happily in the drawing room, enjoying the first of his birthday's we would share together.

Gordon and Margo arrived first, bringing Ruth with them, and explained that they were going out for the evening with her but just wanted to give Rikki his birthday card as they passed. Rikki persuaded them to stay for a drink, and then Clem arrived. By now Rikki was becoming a bit sceptical about a romantic dinner for two, but I was more interested in Ruth, who was looking fabulous in a dress which left nothing to the imagination. She had chosen to sit on a four-seater sofa, and patted the seat next to her for Clem, who was more than happy to join her. They seemed to be getting on famously, but now Rikki knew it was not going to be the night he had expected, so I could introduce Ruth to him as my colleague and friend, and I hoped that she would read from my eyes, 'Don't even think about it, he's *mine.*'

I needn't have worried, because at that point our tall, dark, handsome doctor friend came in. Ruth was at once on her feet, shaking his hand and gazing into his eyes, and then she managed to draw him down on the sofa between Clem and herself. Poor Clem, he obviously knew his turn was over, so consoled himself with another drink and a plateful of nuts and olives. Dick was already bowled over by Ruth, and the rest of us just talked round about them! It couldn't last, of course. Ten minutes later Iain and Sean Connery appeared. Ruth's face was a study, for she had no idea he was going to be there – it had seemed wiser not to mention it. Now the four-seater sofa really became useful, and Ruth ended up there with Dick then Clem on her right, and Sean, as close as she could get to him, on her left.

Dinner was a very leisurely affair, beautifully served by Mrs Wares. Rikki was by now thoroughly enjoying himself and the conversation and laughter filled the room. The wine flowed freely, and only Gordon was being careful because no one but he would be driving. Ruth and Dick were staying the night and Iain's chauffeur would drive him and Sean home, so we were all very mellow when someone decided we should have a game of darts.

Rikki had a games room upstairs with two sets of dart boards and a table tennis table, and that's where his friends would gather in his freedom years. In those days everyone smoked and drank a great deal and the language was choice. A real Boys' Night. When it became too smoky to see the dart boards, they opened the windows wide so that the smoke and the language escaped, and as the windows here opened, all the neighbours shut theirs very firmly. The main concern for the boys was the smoke, in case the fire brigade were called, but no one actually complained, and it was a fairly short-lived experience.

On Rikki's birthday night however, the men were being very polite, there were plenty of drinks around but the air wasn't blue with either smoke or swearing. We played darts for an hour or so, but it was getting late and we were all rather tired, so we returned to the drawing room for a farewell drink. It was only after Rikki and I had poured the drinks and given them to our guests that I realised we had only poured seven drinks, and there were nine of us for the evening. Rikki and I, without saying a word to anyone else, had a quick look around the house, but all the rooms, and the bathrooms were empty. It was only then we realised that Sean and Ruth had never left the games room. We rejoined the group and eventually the missing pair appeared, Sean as immaculate as ever, though Ruth did look a little dishevelled – still with her lovely smile, only slightly spoiled by a total lack of lipstick. They joined us for the nightcap drink, and I'm sure, although no one said a word, that we all hoped they had enjoyed their sojourn in the games room . . .

After some more chat our guests left for home, and all we had to do was show Ruth and Dick their respective bedrooms. Rikki and I couldn't wait to fall into bed, and we agreed that the evening had been something of a surprise.

The surprises didn't end there. In the morning Mrs Wares took up morning tea to our guests, taking tea into Ruth's room first, where she found Dick curled up in bed beside her. Without turning a hair, our dear sophisticated Mrs Wares smilingly wished them good morning and hoped they had had an enjoyable evening and night, and placed Dick's tea on the table at his side of the bed. Now that's style!

I was now working full time with STV and liking it a great deal. In a way the Transmission Control area was a world apart from the main building. It was on the top floor, a long way away from all the studios, and the controllers and their assistants were the nicest men you could meet. I don't remember any rows there, we all seemed to get on with each other – not a situation you come across very often in the world of television. One thing I particularly liked was that the announcers were not in vision, it was all voice over, and I found that relaxing.

It had taken me a while to recover from the only time Rikki saw me working at Tyne Tees. He came to Newcastle for the weekend, and we stayed at a rather nice hotel, called, I think, the Gosforth Park. We settled in there, and I left to go to work on the night shift, leaving Rikki who had decided to have dinner in our room, and then, surprise, surprise, watch television. The announcer's studio in Newcastle was an odd arrangement – it was in the basement, and the control room was on the top floor. In all other studios I had been used to being adjacent to the control room, where you could see the controller, and he could see his announcer, which could be useful if there was any crisis, but here there was only a disembodied voice giving instructions.

The other thing to which I was accustomed was the absence of meal breaks, so if you became hungry you would phone the canteen and they would bring whatever you ordered to your desk. The one thing they all knew was not to enter the studio if the red light on the door was on, because that meant the camera and lights were on and you were in vision. When the camera lights were off there was still enough light to read by but obviously it wasn't so bright. That night all I had ordered was a roast beef sandwich and a glass of milk, which duly arrived. I was actually looking forward to the evening's viewing, and I was sure Rikki would be watching as well. We both liked the 'Saint' books by Leslie Charteris, and the Saint played by Roger Moore was starting at 8.30 that evening. I settled down to enjoy it.

As time passed I thought it was a strangely complicated plot, and you really had to concentrate on it in case you missed something, so I decided that some nourishment might help my brain-power and took a large bite out of my beef sandwich. Looking back at the screen I felt I must have missed something; the scene seemed to have lost Roger Moore and his girlfriend, and was now filming a large desk, behind which was a woman with her mouth full, and oddly enough wearing the same dress as me. Only slowly did the horror of it all dawn on me.

The controller, instead of pressing the button to change the film reel, had by mistake pressed the announcer's studio instead. Rikki said afterwards that my face was a study as I chewed away with interest at what was on the screen and then realised that it was me, and politely stopped chewing, but it was all too late. By the time they got back into the film the plot was lost forever. I could imagine a viewer saying to his wife, 'I'm not sure who the murderer was, but I think it was that woman who was eating all the time.'

Not the best of times for Rikki to have been viewing! For years afterwards I always gave him a quizzical look any time he said, 'How about a roast beef sandwich, darling?'

12

THE BOYS ARE BACK IN TOWN

We were hardly believing our luck. Neither of us had been so happy in our lives, and being so much in love was an experience that it isn't possible to explain.

I was surprised then when Rikki asked me if I was free the following Wednesday. I said I thought so, but what did he have in mind?

He said, 'I thought, we might get married.' And so we did, on 13 August 1969.

Needless to say it wasn't straightforward. We just wanted to turn up at the Registry Office and sign a bit of paper, but of course we had to have two witnesses, so naturally we invited Gordon and Margo, who were kind enough to accept. When Larry Marshall and Kay heard we were to be married they insisted that they should be there, and how could we refuse? Rikki and I had decided that after going to Martha Street the six of us would come home for some champagne and sandwiches, and then having had time to change for dinner we would all meet up again at a restaurant in town, and that's what we did. I did suggest to Rikki that as Larry and Kay were joining us, that we should include them in the marriage ceremony, with the result that we have a quite unique marriage certificate which states – Best Man, Gordon Milne, Best Maid, Henry Tomasso (Larry's real name).

It really was a strange kind of day. I had no idea what a civil marriage was like, but the Registrar and all the staff could not have been more friendly and welcoming, and put us at ease. The only problem occurred when we arrived in Martha Street, where Rikki found a parking space right at the door. What a good omen I thought! It was short-lived, for as usual he had no money whatsoever with him. One press photographer had somehow discovered we were going to be there that afternoon, with the result that the following day our one and only wedding photograph was of Rikki standing over me while I searched frantically through my handbag for change for the meter. Perhaps we brought it on ourselves – we were both wearing green, the date was the thirteenth, and our first wedding present was an opal!

The drive into town came as a big surprise. We had awakened happily, and very lovingly, and were so looking forward to the day ahead, but for some reason when we got into the car we couldn't carry on a conversation. We ended up discussing the weather! I can only think that we were both scared. We each had a failed marriage behind us, and what if we were to ruin the tremendous happiness we now shared by legalising it.

It was only when we returned to the house, and there was dear Mrs Wares saying, 'Welcome home, Mrs Fulton,' that I knew for sure we had got it right, and Rikki felt exactly the same.

We went out with our guests for dinner, which was most enjoyable, and returned home around midnight. It had been quite a day. We sat talking until about 1am, when the door bell rang and there was our good friend Iain, this time without Sean. On his way home to his beautiful house 'Lochbrae' in Bearsden, he often drove past our house in the early hours, after business meetings, and if our lights were on he would ring the bell. It was always a pleasure to see him. However I don't know how many brides and grooms spent their wedding night discussing politics! It's hardly traditional, but then we never were. But we did invite

119

our families for dinner to celebrate our wedding, although not on the same night – we had mine on Thursday, and Rikki's on Friday.

I had been over visiting my parents on the previous Monday, and while my mother was making coffee I asked Daddy if he would come to dinner on Thursday. He opened his mouth to say 'no' but when I quickly added that Rikki and I were marrying on Wednesday, he said he would be very happy to come. As Mummy returned to the room, he said to her that they were going to Rikki's house on Thursday. She was astonished, 'But, Bill, you said you wouldn't set foot . . .' He interrupted her: 'They're getting married on Wednesday.' Her face was a study, the happiness just shining from her expression. It was a moment I treasure.

Our first formal dinner as a married couple could not be called a success.

Mrs Wares and I had decided on duck for the main course. I knew my parents liked it, and I was pretty sure both my sister Doreen and her husband Tom did as well. Unfortunately neither of us thought of mentioning it to Rikki, so when he was presented with the first duck on a platter he thought it was a very miserly turkey, and proceeded to carve it as such. My father, who was an expert carver, couldn't control his laughter, which did nothing to help the situation and the duck fat splattered up the wall, ruining the wallpaper. To make matters worse, Tom and Doreen had kindly brought us a bottle of champagne which they insisted we should have with our meal, but as they had driven from their home in Mugdock the bottle had been well and truly shaken and was no longer chilled, with the result that when Rikki opened it the cork hit the ceiling, followed by most of the champagne. I have to admit that I wasn't at all upset. We were obviously going to have to redecorate the dining room, which had to be a good thing. I had hated the wallpaper, which was what I can only describe as Elastoplast pink, and the sooner it went the better.

Rikki and me in the garden, just after having our marriage blessed.

So near and yet so far. The Mark Gudgeon portraits when we missed each other by two hours

At the Lido in Paris for my 35th birthday

Being interviewed on Grampian Television

Doctor of Letters, at Strathclyde University ...

... and now Doctor Doctor of Letters, at the University of St. Andrews

A pyjama party for Rikki's 65th birthday

With Duguld and Maggie Jaffray on the evening before our Silver Wedding Anniversary

The real supercops with their favourite recruit

Jake on his favourite window seat

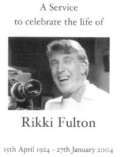

A Service
to celebrate the life of

Rikki Fulton

15th April 1924 - 27th January 2004

Clydebank Crematorium
3rd February 2004
3.30pm

Conducted by:
The Revd. Alastair H. Symington MA, BD

Tribute by:
Mr Tony Roper

The way we were

The way we are

To my beloved Rikki,

With Love – all of it!
On our special anniversary, thank you
for being the most wonderful husband
anyone could ever have.
You transformed my life when we met in
Aberdeen, and I am so incredibly lucky and
proud to be your wife. Through all
eternity, I love you,
              Kate.

Our last anniversary

The following night we had Rikki's two brothers and their wives for dinner. I liked both John and Jim. John, who had been divorced many years ago, made a surprise visit to Rikki one Sunday and announced, 'I'm thinking of getting married again, do you think I'm stupid?' Rikki was very reassuring and wished him every happiness. The two of them then settled down to watch the Sunday film, which was *Random Harvest*, a tear-jerker to end them all. Rikki had carefully made sure that he sat behind John, because he knew how the film would affect him, and he didn't want his big brother to catch him crying! As it turned out both of them were in floods of tears at the end of the film, and John managed, in a strangled voice, to say, 'They don't make them like that any more.' He married his charming wife Ann in January 1969, and she looked after him magnificently for the rest of his life. As did Margaret for Jim. They were the only members of the Fulton family to have children, and Stuart and Glynis are a real credit to them.

It made me realise what a powerful mother the Fulton fellows must have had. She had done absolutely everything for them, and the three of them assumed that all women were like her. Luckily for them, the wives they chose loved them to bits, and wanted to take care of them. I'm sure their mother would have approved. How I wish I had met her, and though it might have been daunting I'm sure she could have taught me a great deal.

Having got our marriage well and truly established Rikki and I were able to relax, and once again just enjoy being together. A few things changed at home. Sometimes on days when I wasn't working I would do the cooking, and occasionally phoned our order to the grocer, which meant Mrs Wares and I waged our silent war over the butter. If I had ordered, the bright yellow salted would appear, only to be ignored by Mrs Wares, who would at once phone for the pure white unsalted, which was the only one she would use. Never a word was spoken.

The one thing neither Rikki nor I had thought about was a

honeymoon. We certainly couldn't go abroad and leave the dogs, but we had heard of a Highland hotel which preferred canines to humans, and that sounded just right for the four of us. So off we went.

We had a lovely drive north, with the dogs behaving perfectly, and when we arrived they were welcomed with open arms, and asked to fill in the form with the humans they were bringing with them. It was unfortunate that Jonathon had never learned how to spell, and Jeeves, who, as always, knew everything, was fast asleep. On their behalf we filled in the necessary form, and went to unpack. The dogs were given every freedom in the hotel, except of course not being allowed in the dining room, and when I explained to Jeeves that really this could be called our honeymoon, he looked most impressed, and obviously made a mental note that honeymoons are a very good thing for dogs to go on!

Going there was like stepping into a Somerset Maugham novel. The owners were decidedly upper class and delightfully eccentric. The hotel was very comfortably old-fashioned, and I wondered what had made the owners buy it. I wouldn't be at all surprised if they had stayed there, liked it, and instead of going home, bought it.

Her name was Bunty and his was James, and they spent most of the time arguing in both the kitchen and dining room – often fixing back the kitchen door so that they, and we, could hear every word. The rows usually involved a third man and James explained to us that this philanderer 'is very fond of Bunty, in fact sometimes he's *too* fond of Bunty!' Mealtimes were never dull. There was a most attractive lady who was in the foyer selling cashmere sweaters, and sometimes the tables would turn, and Bunty would accuse James of indiscretions with this lady. When they weren't rowing they seemed to get on famously.

We enjoyed walking the dogs through the tiny village to get to the glorious woods beyond, where they had the most marvellous time, trying to leave no tree untouched, though after about ten minutes they were both miming and we pretended to be impressed.

The day before we left, Rikki wanted to fill the car up with petrol so we drove to the only garage, which was very close to the hotel. There we met a most delightful man, possibly in his late thirties, good-looking, with a lovely speaking voice. We didn't know if he was the garage owner or whether he just worked there, but he couldn't have been more polite or helpful. At lunch that day we told James how impressed we were with his manners and helpfulness.

'Ah yes,' said James knowledgeably. 'That's Patrick, he's an unfrocked priest – and he's another one that's very fond of Bunty.'

We drove home feeling rather stunned. We truly did not know how the other half live. The fun and games in that Highland village made *Eastenders* look like a children's fairy tale. Maybe that's the answer – perhaps if we tried to find it again, like Brigadoon, it would have vanished for another hundred years. We arrived home in plenty of time for Rikki and Jack to start rehearsing for the Pavilion pantomime. They both seemed so happy to be working together again; they had both had a bad time professionally but it did feel as though their good days were returning. As always they worked very hard on their material, and it certainly paid off. The pantomime *Francie and Josie in Wonderland*, was in Rikki's opinion, an astonishing success. It seemed that Glasgow was delighted to have 'The Boys' back, and they were more than happy to be back.

Pantomime is incredibly hard work. Even the costume changes can be exhausting, some are so very heavy to wear, and the stars of the show never have a chance to relax in their dressing rooms; from the moment the curtain goes up they are either on stage or clambering into their next costume. Good audiences made all the difference, especially for Rikki and Jack, because so much of their comedy was born in front of an audience. The popular 'Arbroath' gag was originally written as a two-minute joke, but there was such a good audience reaction that the boys enjoyed playing up to it, and it lasted for twenty minutes. The audience loved it, Francie and Josie loved it, the time-conscious stage manager did not!

I don't think they ever gave the same performance two nights running. It was part of the magic, and you could be sure you would go home having seen or heard something that no other audience had.

After the long season at the Pavilion, Rikki and Jack had only a few weeks to relax before they were off to take Francie and Josie to Ulster. The television station had always shown the original series, and they were as popular there as they were at home, and the audiences were wildly enthusiastic. The first week there they did a series of one-night stands, one of which impressed Rikki tremendously. It was in the church hall in Ballymoney. The priest had invited all his parishioners to an evening meal there, to be followed by entertainment from Francie and Josie, and then a light supper with wine. Rikki was most impressed, and said to the priest, 'Father, a day like this must be tremendously expensive. How do you manage to pay for it?'

The priest put down his gin and tonic, and whispered in Rikki's ear, 'You should see how much I take off them at the bingo!'

The following week Jack's wife Mary and I joined our husbands, and we had a most happy time in Belfast. One night at the Grove Theatre the Ballymoney priest appeared in the bar after the show, and as Rikki laid a gin and tonic down for him, he asked him the question he always asked the clergy: 'Why should I believe in God?' The priest replied, 'Why Not?' The most succinct answer ever! Then he and Rikki settled down to discuss theology until dawn.

There was only a brief pause before F and J were off on an

124

extensive tour of Scotland, perhaps to confirm to themselves that they really were back. By the time they were reassured they were also exhausted, and Rikki still had to write that year's pantomime for the Pavilion.

Enough was enough, and we decided a holiday in the sun would do us a world of good. Not surprisingly we chose Majorca. It wasn't far from home, and it had sea and sun, what more could we ask? This time, however, it was a little different, because we invited Gordon and Margo to be our guests. What a good idea that turned out to be! We had a wonderful time, all four of us in a second honeymoon mood! This time we didn't go to Pollensa, but on our travel agent's advice to Cala Mayor, where we stayed at the Santa Ana hotel, which we liked. We found the staff very friendly and enjoyed long chats with the head waiter, Mateo, and we were most surprised and delighted when he invited us to his home. This really was most unexpected, as Spaniards and Majorcans rarely invite strangers into their houses. We felt honoured, and determined to observe Spanish etiquette, whatever it might be!

We had been invited for a Spanish afternoon tea, and not having the faintest idea what that would be, we decided not to have lunch in case we couldn't do justice to the sandwiches and cake. Our host Mateo sent a car for us, and as we were driven in the sunshine through the beautiful tree-lined glades to his village, I thought, I must always remember today.

The village consisted of one street with houses on either side, and with the flowers and tables and chairs outside, it looked so welcoming. One of Mateo's daughters had recently been married there, and he showed us the wedding photographs. After the marriage ceremony the reception was traditional, the whole village being invited, and the meal was served on tables in the street. Can't see it happening in Bearsden!

Mateo and his wife Maria were on the doorstep when we arrived and could not have been more hospitable. Conversation was not easy. Maria spoke no English, and Rikki was the only one who attempted Spanish, but the day was saved by Mateo, who with his restaurant languages could cope with anything.

We were ushered into the front room for the afternoon tea, something we were now longing for as we were all famished, but as we went in, we became silent.

There was a large table completely covered in liqueur bottles. Not a morsel of food in sight.

We were offered Grand Marnier to start with, followed by every liqueur we had heard of and quite a few we hadn't. Our hunger seemed to have been replaced, due to the vast amount of liquid we were consuming, but unfortunately we were losing the ability to move. Slowly it dawned on us, one by one, that the only word to describe ourselves was 'paralytic'. Fortunately Mateo was going to drive us back to the hotel, where he would be serving dinner, and I'm sure he was not at all surprised that none of us appeared again that night. Ever since then when I am being served, or serving, cucumber sandwiches and cream scones, I remember that afternoon and think wistfully that the Majorcans have more fun.

On our flight home we were saying how much we had enjoyed the holiday, and Rikki was already making reassuring noises about the following year. However, we decided to be practical and that we should all help to finance the next trip. For some time the four of us had been playing canasta, so from now on, until our next holiday, we would play for money, and it would all go into a Majorcan kitty.

It seemed we were only just home when Rikki and Jack started work on their next pantomime. It was to be *The Magic of Francie and Josie* at the Pavilion directed by one of Rikki's favourite people. He kept a note of all the pantomimes he had done, and of their directors, so this year it read, 'Directed by dear Max Norris'. Max was an exceptional man, who had a lifetime of show business behind him, and there was nothing he didn't know about comedy. He was wonderful company and he left many sad friends when he died.

The festive season always passed in a whirl though we enjoyed it, but being the busiest time of the year for Rikki, I tried not to bother him with decorations in the house, or the Christmas tree. In fact it became a tradition that I would put up the tree and put the lights on it, so that one night when Rikki drove home it would be shining in the window, but he never knew which night it would be. He did insist though on taking it down, because he thought, quite rightly, that no one could put away the tree and lights as neatly as he could.

One year, however, things did not go as planned. I got the tree out of its box (I must admit we always had artificial ones) set it up in the drawing-room window and collected all the decorations for it – an easy task because they had been carefully packed away. Having dressed the tree, all I needed was the lights. I searched the house from top to bottom with no success. The lights were nowhere to be found. I couldn't understand it – Rikki was always so careful when the Christmas tree and decorations were put away for the year. I just had to admit defeat. There just had to be an answer – he couldn't come home to a tree in darkness.

There used to be a wonderful ironmonger's in Byres Road, I think it was called Tulleys, and we were regular customers. In a last-minute attempt to save the day, or rather the night, I phoned to see if they had fairy lights. Not only did they have them, but they brought them to the house and dressed the tree with them! How I blessed their Christmas goodwill. Rikki came home to a sparkling tree.

It was only when he was carefully packing the tree and decorations away that I told him these were new lights, and the old ones were lost. As I knew he would, he tore the house apart looking for them, to no avail. The mystery remained. There is a small room at the very back of the house which was originally a wash house, and Rikki had had it shelved. People kindly called it a work room, we called it the coup. Some years after 1970, I went through there for a pair of pliers, and for the first time noticed a row of box files on the top shelf, neatly arranged, and the one which caught my eye said 'Fairy Lights'. He had filed the fairy lights! You can't get much tidier than that.

No sooner had Rikki and Jack finished pantomime than they were doing a spring season in Ayr, followed by a sell-out visit to Dundee. It did seem as though the 'boys were back in town', and no one was happier about that than the Boys themselves. They were going to have a much-needed break in May, but I had no idea what form it would take. I soon learned. Rikki was going to take me to Paris for my 35th birthday.

We had a glorious time, and did all the things that tourists are supposed to do. We saw the wonderful paintings in the Louvre, we went to Napoleon's tomb, where Rikki showed me that to get a view of it you had to lean over the gallery, which meant that to see it, you had to bow to the Emperor. On my birthday we went to the Lido for dinner and very much enjoyed the fabulous cabaret. The following night we went to Maxim's for dinner, mainly because I wanted to be sure it really existed, and wasn't just a figment of Hollywood's imagination. When we saw the prices of the menu, we knew for sure it was real! Not that that would have bothered the party at the table next to us – the hostess was Coco Chanel.

We did have a minor disaster there. Behind our table was a glass screen and when a waiter bumped into it, it started to fall over me, I twisted round and caught it in time, so there was no harm done, at least not to the screen, but the zip on my evening dress came apart. Rikki was on his feet in a second, and refusing all the help offered by Maxim's staff, tried to get the zip together. Somehow or other he managed it, and we were able to enjoy the rest of our meal. We were just finishing our coffee when the zip went for the second time. Without a flicker of unease, Rikki asked for the bill, and having paid it, told me to stay absolutely still until he returned. This I did, and when he came back he had collected my velvet evening cloak which with a magnificent gesture he swung around my shoulders. We sailed out of Maxims, reached the Champs Élysées and my dress fell off!

When we arrived back at our hotel, which for some reason was called 'The Oxford and Cambridge', we found an English couple there who were totally bewildered. I imagine they chose that particular hotel because they assumed everyone there would speak English, but they didn't. Not one of the staff could help. I stood a little distance away and tried desperately to remember what Mr Conrad had taught me in my teens. When I did summon up the courage to attempt to speak, it was too late. Rikki had signed the visitors' book for them, and was now showing them to their room accompanied by the porter with whom he was deep in conversation. He never ceased to amaze me; he had sorted out all the problems, and he couldn't speak a word of French! He started to learn it when we got home.

Once back, Rikki had to start writing that year's pantomime for the Pavilion, and by the time he finished that, it was time for our Majorcan holiday. We were all so looking forward to it, and arrived at the airport clutching our canasta kitty. We were all determined to make sure that it wouldn't be squandered, but only spent on essential things, like brandy and champagne! It was lovely to be back in the sunshine, and in the hotel we had liked so much, but very sadly the magic had gone. I've never understood why. It was obvious that Gordon and Margo weren't enjoying it nearly as much as the year before, and perhaps we were expecting too much. You daydream about a place, but in reality it can't match your dreams. Rikki and I decided we would not return to Cala Mayor, and we never did. It was a pity it ended not with a bang, but a whimper.

The winter followed its usual pattern. Rikki would be working very hard and needed as much rest as he could possibly get. He arrived home just before midnight, and as he enjoyed his brandy, he would come through to the kitchen to tell me how the show had gone, while I served our main meal of the day. This we would have in front of the fire in the drawing room, talking non-stop as always. After finishing our meal we took the dogs out for their walk, invariably losing Jonathon, who loved exploring, while Jeeves wasn't nearly as adventurous and preferred to stay with us. At first we used to worry when we couldn't find Jonathon, but he soon taught us that when we arrived back at the house, he would be waiting in the porch, and he always was.

In the spring we were invited to a party in a very nice house in Milngavie. There were many guests, and in those days every-one smoked, so it reached a stage where you couldn't see to whom you were speaking because the air was so blue. When we got home Rikki took out his cigarettes and threw them in the bin. 'I'm never going to smoke again,' he said, and didn't. There were no half measures with Rikki! He had never been a heavy smoker, only about eight to ten a day, but he did enjoy smoking while he was writing, but, having made up his mind, that was it.

13

FROM JOSIE TO SHAKESPEARE

We had decided to have an early holiday in '72. But where to go? As usual Rikki had the answer. In the spring of the year we met, he had taken a holiday on his own in Barbados which he much enjoyed and he wanted to show the island to me. It didn't take much persuasion. We stayed in a lovely hotel, right on the beach. In those days it was called The Miramar, but I believe it's now called The Royal Pavilion. There was only one other couple from Britain there, a most elegant pair, beautifully dressed and never a hair out of place. After two days we reached the stage of smiling to each other, but I felt to start a conversation would have been an intrusion. When Rikki and I were on holiday we carefully didn't follow the news, no phones, no radio, no newspapers. We were seriously there to enjoy ourselves.

It therefore came as a surprise when one morning at breakfast a beautifully elocuted female voice asked: 'Did you know the Duke of Windsor has died?'

That certainly broke the ice, and we chatted happily for the rest of our holiday. Their name was Forrester, he was a lawyer, and they lived in Royal Crescent, Bath. What a perfect setting for them. I wondered if they had received the news of the Duke's death privately from the royal family, but perhaps it was only the radio.

Breakfast was always marvellous. The dining room was outdoors in the delightful sunshine, and birds would come to the table to be fed. If you were mean and didn't give them anything they didn't hold a grudge, they just ate the sugar out of the bowl instead. They were tiny, but every colour you can think of. An azure bird landed on the table and I asked our waiter, 'What kind of bird is that?' He replied knowledgeably, 'That's a blue bird,' and when I asked about a canary-coloured bird he said, 'That's a yellow bird.' I felt I was beginning to understand, so that when a very dark bird landed I said, 'Don't tell me, that's a black bird, isn't it?' The waiter nodded with relief. My lesson in ornithology was over!

For once Rikki wasn't longing to get home, we were liking Barbados so much. It was a completely different lifestyle. We used to walk along the deserted beach, hand in hand, talking to the sand crabs at 6.30 in the morning, before joining the birds for breakfast. Often we would walk into town, which apparently was unusual – nobody walked, they drove – but we loved a stroll in the sunshine and the chance to pass the time of day with the people who lived there. One morning an extremely stout black lady waved to us from the other side of the road, and when we stopped she came over with an outsize grin for Rikki, and asked me, 'Honey, going to zip my dress for me?' She turned around and her dress was wide open from just above the hem to her neck. I wondered if she had to wait each morning for crazy visitors to walk past her home before she could go into town, and when I zipped her, we were obviously friends for life. It was all so casual and peaceful, and quite the best holiday we had ever had.

Arriving home was a little different too. Rikki was asked to join the Lyceum Theatre Company with Bill Bryden as director. He absolutely loved it – one minute he was playing Josie, and the next, Malvolio in Shakespeare's *Twelfth Night*. He gave a wonderful, and as you might imagine, very original performance as Malvolio. Shortly after that he discovered the playwright he admired above them all, when he played in Molière's *The Miser*. He and Molière shared a real love affair that went on for years.

His next role was Flatterie in *The Three Estates* at the Edinburgh Festival, (I was happy that he kept my good-luck card – 'This time, flatterie will get you somewhere'). It was a dual role because Flatterie was also the Pardoner who could dispense divorces. As he finished the divorce speech he looked straight into the audience, and one night was startled to find one of them staring straight back at him. It was Ethel! She was there with her husband the Procurator Fiscal, and the Law Society. They didn't go backstage!

After all the straight acting Rikki was quite happy to be back in pantomime. This year he was at the King's Theatre, Edinburgh, with *Robinson Crusoe* and a cast of Walter Carr, Una MacLean, and Larry Marshall. I was concerned that not only did Rikki have the pressure of the show to cope with but he also did all the driving. He reassured me that he found the drive home relaxing, and I was so glad that Una and Larry were with him. The director, Clive Perry, was a newcomer to us, but in a short time he became, and is, a very good friend. It was the first time in years that Rikki led the show himself. He and Jack had become so used to working together, but it seems inevitable that after a time relationships become strained, and it was very wise of them to take a break and remain close friends.

As Rikki rested after a good but tiring season, we started to think of where we should go on holiday, and as always came to the same conclusion. We didn't want our last visit to spoil the whole of Majorca for us so we would go back to the north of the island which we had so enjoyed. We went to the same hotel, which was right in the centre of Puerto de Pollensa next to the harbour which was always fascinating.

This year we explored a little more, and discovered the place where all the Scots gathered. It was called Katy's Bar, and many people asked if it was mine. If only!! I had to explain that in

Spanish Katy is pronounced catty. We very much enjoyed meeting fellow Scots, most of whom were ex-pats who had retired there and couldn't wait to hear what was going on at 'home'. Some of them we came to know well, and we promised to get in touch with them next time we were there.

Back home Rikki was straight into a production of *Benny Lynch*, a play about the world-champion boxer and his sad life. Rikki was playing his manager, and the play was at the Pavilion, Glasgow. One Friday night when he came home we were discussing buying some things for the breakfast room and he was most enthusiastic about it, insisting that we go to Byres Road in the morning and see what we would like. When I pointed out to him that he had a matinée that day he laughed and said we would have plenty of time before that. So off we went, scouring many shops and finding some of the bits and pieces we were looking for. Around noon I noticed that Rikki was looking rather pale, and at once insisted that it was time to go home for lunch. He had no objection.

I had to help him out of the car and into the house where he collapsed into a chair saying he felt ill. He didn't want any lunch, but dozed off in his chair. I was in a quandary – should I let him sleep or make him wake up? Eventually I decided. It took some time to get him upright, and even longer to get him into the car, but once he was there I relaxed. He didn't. All the way into town he shouted, 'What are you doing to me, I'm not well enough to do the play.' I explained as calmly as I could that we were going to the theatre, not for him to go onstage but to get a doctor. On a Saturday afternoon it would be a locum doctor who came to the house, with no knowledge of Rikki's health, and I knew from experience that a theatre doctor would be there in minutes.

Phil Macoll, who was in the cast, came into Rikki's dressing room and we managed to get him flat on the floor, covered in blankets – Rikki, that is, not Phil. What I was afraid of, was that he was having a heart attack, and when the young doctor arrived he seemed to think the same. That really scared me, especially when he sent for an ambulance to take Rikki to the Royal Infirmary in Glasgow.

I followed in my car, and thankfully by the time I found him in the hospital they had already decided that there was nothing wrong with his heart. He was suffering from hyperglycemia and needed to have a massive intake of sugar. This they gave him in tumblers of lemonade filled up with glucose. The result was astonishing, in a very short time Rikki's colour began to come back to his face, and he sounded like a human being again. It was unbelievably wonderful to have him back again!

The doctors said he must go straight home to bed and continue with the lemonade and glucose, which they kindly gave me to take away. I was so grateful to them. In an hour they had removed every problem, and left us with the excellent news that Rikki had a very good heart. I'd always known that, but it was reassuring to know that it was also good physically! Fortunately with the next day being Sunday, there was plenty of time for him to rest and recover, and be only too glad to return to work on Monday.

Rikki had only a short break before his next Lyceum production, which was a play about the troubles in Northern Ireland. It all revolved around one family where the father and son had conflicting loyalties. Rikki played a friend of the family, who could only be called 'perjink'. He was very polite, teetotal, a regular churchgoer and he lived alone leading a very dull life. Jan Wilson was playing the mother, and when Rikki made his entrance, on cue she handed him a glass of orange juice which he took, saying, 'That's a terrible drink to give to a Catholic.' The audience laughed, but there was a slight pause onstage. Neither the cast nor Rikki had ever heard that line before. Jan was wonderful, smiling at him, and continuing with the words that had been scripted, but then she was lucky – having worked with

Rikki in pantomime she knew you could never be sure what he was going to say next!

There was a lot of comedy before Rikki made his exit, and this continued for some time and then developed into a party, by which time all the characters were pretty drunk. There was a tremendous amount of laughter and they all started singing and dancing. Into this happy crowd returned Rikki, but as a quite different man. He was pale, he held on to the furniture and staggered a little, no one could make out what he was saying they were making so much noise, and they were suggesting to each other that the teetotaller had come off the wagon. But eventually they stopped to listen and Rikki had a most moving speech to say that he had just seen one of their menfolk killed. The curtain came down on that first act of the play to utter silence. Even when the lights came on in the auditorium no one moved. Then there was some self-conscious murmuring, the handkerchiefs came out, and the audience sought solace in the bars. Just what the producer had hoped for!

That year, 1974, we returned to Pollensa where it was lovely to meet again the friends we had met the previous year, but this time we stayed in a different hotel. It was round the bay from the town centre and right on the beach so we were swimming in the sea which we both preferred to a pool, and the walk into town couldn't have been better. They call it the Pine walk, and it was heaven to stroll along there in the glorious sunshine with the blue of the sea on one side and the green of the trees on the other. We walked into town at least twice a day convincing ourselves that it was doing us good getting the exercise. Absolute nonsense! We did it because we loved it.

On our morning walk we made sure we always went past the cleaners where there was such a funny thing they used to do, and this wasn't only in Majorca, we saw it also on the mainland. The Majorcans are excellent cleaners but they are also expert window dressers and they do like colour, so if your dress is left to be cleaned and they like it, until it is collected they will have it in the front of their window display. Embarrassing if you never spotted any of your clothes there as you could lose faith in your fashion sense!

The other great advantage of our new hotel was that we met two people who became friends for life. They were Dr Gilbert Hope and his wife, Jenny. Gilbert was the doctor in Coupar Angus, and they lived in 'The Old Manse' quite nearby. It was an enchanting house with grounds that went right down to the loch. We spent many happy weekends there, and we loved it when they came to us.

One thing that made our time together so special was that we all loved to play bridge, but very much 'Fireside Bridge', which involved a great deal of laughter. I find it so fortunate that four people can meet unexpectedly and without exception like each other, and that's the way it was.

We were heartbroken when Gilbert died; he was one of the finest men I have ever met, but how lucky he was to have found Jenny. She was incredibly brave but it must have been shattering for her. She decided to leave The Old Manse, and then one really nice thing happened. Their son who was a doctor in America said he was coming home with his wife and sons. Not only that, he bought The Old Manse, and now replaces Gilbert as the doctor for the same area.

Meeting the Hopes just made our holiday, and we looked forward to seeing them in Scotland, but it did make us think about holidays. We were now so besotted by Pollensa that we were afraid of getting into a rut, so we made up our minds that the following year we would go somewhere else. Having reached that momentous decision we came home to Glasgow.

That winter was a little easier for Rikki because the production and cast of the Edinburgh production came through to Glasgow, and he didn't have to write a script for once. The pantomime, *Robinson Crusoe*, had the usual long run, and it seemed to be a happy season. Shortly after Rikki had had a very brief rest, he was to be in another production of *God is Good* and when that ended he was in need of a well-earned, proper break.

We had spent a lot of time on our nightly dog walks trying to decide where our next holiday should be. We wanted to go somewhere neither of us had been before, and to have sunshine, sea, and a good hotel. We thought of a few places, but in the end we chose the Seychelles. We went there in May, while Mr and Mrs Wares as usual stayed in the house to spare the dogs going to kennels, something both we and the dogs greatly appreciated.

Rikki hated travelling, but when we arrived, even he thought it was worth it. No wonder they call it 'The Isle of Love'. It was breathtakingly beautiful, and we thought we were going to have the holiday of a lifetime. The hotel was excellent, it was right on its own private beach, our room was charming and the food was excellent. The only thing we found a little odd was that although the staff in the restaurant were efficient and courteous, they were very reserved – in fact, they didn't give the impression of being friendly.

There were no waiters, only waitresses, and practically all of them were clearly pregnant. I wondered if that was deliberate, so they would have somewhere to rest their trays . . . We certainly weren't going to waste time trying to find out. We were far too busy lying on the beach with our books enjoying the sunshine. The only snag about that was the begging that went on, tiny children would ask for money, but as there was no point whatsoever in taking money to a beach, we didn't have any. The staff of the hotel quickly sent the beggars packing if they saw them; it was, after all, a private beach and there were even armed guards at the far ends of the beach to dissuade intruders.

There was one old man, however, who managed to get in each day – maybe he was related to one of the guards. I have never seen anyone look as thin as he was. He looked like a walking skeleton and would stand in front of you and mime. First he would point to his concave stomach then to his open mouth, make a pleading gesture and hold out his hands for money. If there was no result he would try it twice more, then resort to language. 'What do you speak?' he would ask in about every language known to man. Rikki and I looked at each other and held a completely silent conversation using only our eyebrows and gazing deeply into each other's eyes. Having reached the same conclusion, I smiled at the old rascal and said 'Gaelic'. He looked puzzled and tried to repeat it unsuccessfully, so in order to be helpful I spoke to him in the only Gaelic I knew. This was David Stuart's speech to the audiences at the end of the plays on the Highland tour. What I said to him was, 'Thank you very much for coming, you've been a lovely audience, I hope we meet again. Goodnight and safe home.' Then we returned to our books.

The following day as we went on our walk we were very pleased to see a 'kent' face. It belonged to a young man we had met on the plane coming over. He was staying in a different hotel, and we asked how he liked it. He told us the hotel was all right, but he was hating the island. We were surprised, so he explained. He had met a couple in his hotel who told him they couldn't believe the poverty the working people lived in – according to them most people still lived in caves. They told him where they were, and he went to see for himself. He said it was quite true, and we should go and see them. Not relishing the idea, we said we would have a look before we went home. That night we saw the waitresses in a rather different light.

Our curiosity got the better of us and next morning we went to see for ourselves. Sure enough the caves were there, and though empty, were obviously lived in. They were all furnished in the same way, the sofa was invariably the back seat of an old car and the armchairs were the front seats. That was all we could see, but it was enough. As we walked back we wondered how these women could reconcile their way of life with the luxury of the hotels they worked in. It must have been intolerable.

139

The other horror story was that though so many women were pregnant, very few were married. Apparently the fathers of the offspring were usually members of the woman's own family. The men didn't work if they could avoid it, but sent the women out to earn some money.

The one thing the men did do was fishing. It was fascinating to watch, and very much a team effort. They would cast enormous nets in the sea around the bay and then the lookouts would climb to the very top of the palm trees, from where – with the perfectly clear water – they could see when a shoal of fish was coming in. When they saw one they shouted their heads off and the nets would be hauled in, brimming with fish. Within minutes they would be divided according to type and size and dispatched to the nearest selling point. The only ones they didn't send were the poisonous Puffer fish. Most of them were thrown back, but there were always one or two left on the beach, covered lightly by sand. The unwary tourist who was unlucky enough to tread on one would know all about it! The pain was agonising, but worst of all they wouldn't be able to walk for weeks afterwards.

Needless to say, from the word go Rikki and I fell in love with a local dog. There were quite a few of them who seemed to have no owners, and fended for themselves. We were adopted by one of them, the cutest mongrel we had ever seen. He made it clear from the start what he wanted, and we were only too happy to obey, with the result that each evening after dinner we would go for our evening walk to be met by our four-legged friend who wondered if by any chance we happened to have a 'doggy bag' with us. He would then have his meal and accompany us on the rest of our walk. We loved it! What did worry me though was that when we left, who would feed him? I decided I would worry about that when the time came.

Meanwhile we just concentrated on enjoying the sun, the sea, the hotel, our books, and most of all each other.

There was rather a lot of interest shown on the beach one

afternoon, when a most attractive young woman appeared with a good-looking escort. They had obviously just arrived. She was outstandingly attractive, but it wasn't just her looks, there was that indefinable quality that makes some people stand out from the crowd. When I said to Rikki that I was sure I had seen her before, he smiled gently, and said: 'You most certainly have, every night on television, on the BBC News. She's Sue Lawley.' Everyone from Britain must have recognised her, but she must have been relieved that no one intruded on them. There was a rumour that they were on their honeymoon, so perhaps that helped guard their privacy!

One morning Rikki and I were strolling back to the hotel for lunch, and they were doing the same, though they were a long way in front of us. As we watched, one of the dogs of the mongrel pack went over to them, and they gave him such a welcome that I thought perhaps she could be the answer to a prayer. And she was! When I explained about the 'doggy bag supper', she said she would give it to him when we left. What a lovely lady.

At this point I should confess that Rikki and I were discovering that we were in fact incompatible on holiday. Although he usually enjoyed it once he got there, he so hated the travelling, hated airports, hated leaving home, and missed the dogs. I love to see new places, meet different people and be looked after in hotels, but I, too, miss the dogs. The result was that I was happy to arrive, Rikki was not. We'd settle in and halfway through the holiday I'd begin to be sad that it would soon be over, but Rikki would become happier and happier because he'd soon be home. So the very start and finish of a holiday were poor but we really enjoyed the bit in-between!

The one invaluable thing the Seychelles had shown us was that Pollensa was definitely going to be our holiday destination from now on.

14

A PIECE OF POLLENSA

In June there was yet another production of *God is Good*, followed by rehearsals for the Edinburgh Festival. I think the full title of the play was *How Mad Tulloch Was Taken Away*, but everyone just called it *Tulloch*. It was a play about the army, and Rikki couldn't have been happier to be in it. He was working with the chums again, and I think he loved being back in uniform. Especially as it was an army one and not naval, so he was unlikely to be torpedoed again as he was during the war. I have a photograph of Rikki and his fellow actor and friend, Billy Armour, and I have never been able to work out whether it was taken on or off stage. Not that it matters – they just look as though they were enjoying themselves, and I'm sure they were.

That was 1976, a memorable year for us. Rikki had a wonderful time doing a comedy season at the Lyceum in Edinburgh produced by Clive Perry. The season began with *The Happiest Days of Your Life*, then Alan Ayckbourn's *Relatively Speaking* and ended with the Feydeau farce, *A Flea in her Ear*. The last one was something of a marathon for Rikki as he was playing two parts in it: he had to run up a steep spiral staircase dressed as a servant, and with the quickest costume change, appear on stage as a successful businessman seconds later. This all worked perfectly, but it certainly took its toll on Rikki's legs. When he came home each night and took the dogs out, for

Rikki it was more of a limp than a walk.

About the same time I became slightly concerned with my own health. I wasn't unwell, just a bit off-colour, and my self-diagnosis was an early menopause, so I dutifully took myself to the doctor, who confirmed there was nothing wrong with my health.

Our friend Iain Stewart still often visited us late at night, if he was out for dinner or in town for a business meeting. Arriving home from the late shift at around half-past one in the morning I was delighted and not at all surprised to see his car at the gate. This meant that Rikki would have been talking politics instead of feeling lonely. He really enjoyed friends coming to the house, so I couldn't understand why he didn't seem as relaxed as usual. He kept insisting that I go to the kitchen and make myself something to eat. When I told him I wasn't very hungry, he began to get annoyed, so thinking that perhaps they had something private to discuss, I dutifully went through to scramble some eggs. When I returned with the eggs and toast, Iain was just about to leave, and when we were alone I assumed it would be like every other night, pouring some wine and discussing the kind of day we had each had. But that night was different; Rikki seemed to be on edge for some reason. When I asked him why he had been so adamant about my having some supper, he replied slowly and very clearly, 'You must, you are eating for two now!'

I could only stare at him. It was so typical of our relationship that Rikki was telling me I was pregnant, instead of my telling him we were going to have a baby. We were both shattered by the news; it was something we hadn't talked about in depth, mainly because between us there was no paternal or maternal instinct. The only time I looked at a pram was if there was a dog tied to it.

We were going to have to reorganise our lives now we were to become a threesome. For days afterwards we really couldn't believe what was happening, and decided we would think about it all in eight months time. Then the doctors discovered I was already twelve weeks' pregnant, which came as a bit of a shock, and made us realise that we had to take the situation seriously. It was a gradual process and we both reacted in exactly the same way, so by the time we had talked it all through in depth we began to quite like the idea. In fact, we became so excited that we were behaving like geriatric teenagers! Telling my parents, I felt my father was slightly lacking in enthusiasm, but my mother more than made up for it!

We had been invited to the Palace of Holyrood for a concert followed by a reception with Her Majesty the Queen, His Royal Highness the Duke of Edinburgh, and Her Royal Highness the Princess Anne. We were both looking forward to it and my father was most impressed, far more than he was with the thought of a third grandchild, especially as he already had two from my sister, and when you've seen one . . .

The next week Daddy had a phone call from Neilson Peterkin, his delightful minister, with whom he had a tough time explaining my living arrangements in Pimlico when he first came to Broom Church, but surely this time there couldn't be a problem. Rikki and I were respectably married, and I was expecting our first child. Neilson had just heard about it and had very kindly phoned with congratulations. When Daddy answered the phone Neilson said, 'I've just heard the wonderful news about Rikki and Kate, do congratulate them for me,' and Daddy who could only think of the following night when we were going to Holyrood said, 'Thank you, Neilson, yes, it is wonderful. Of course Rikki has done it many times before, but it's the first time for Kate. Still I'm sure with all Rikki's experience he'll show her what to do and she will be quite relaxed!' He left a rather bemused minister at the end of the brief phone call.

The next evening we went through to Edinburgh. The music was to be provided by The Baroque Ensemble, of which Prince

Philip was the patron. The room was large, though I doubt if there were as many as 200 guests and there was a dais in the centre where the musicians would play, with chairs arranged around it. Everyone had arrived punctually and it felt rather like being in church. Everyone whispered, and most sat on the edge of their seats. It was all rather tense, until all hell broke loose. There was a long corridor which led into the music room from the royal apartments and charging down it came the corgis barking their heads off, racing around the dais several times and just moments before the royal family arrived went back to their quarters. It was the best possible ice-breaker, so that when the royal party appeared their guests were still laughing and thoroughly enjoying themselves. The concert was as you would expect quite excellent, and after it we were shown into another room where the reception was to be held. Everyone was presented to the three members of the royal family and they then each joined groups of guests just to chat.

We were with Prince Philip who was regaling us with the information as to how sausage skins are manufactured. He had been shown round a sausage factory that morning and was most impressed with it. I realised that Rikki was not giving his entire concentration to this culinary lecture. He had just seen the Queen join the group next to us, their eyes met, and to my astonishment Rikki smiled at her, nodded his head and winked! I couldn't believe it, and hissed at him, 'You have just given Her Majesty the Queen the nod,' but the extraordinary thing was that with sparkling eyes she returned the smile *and* the nod, but drew a line at the wink!

The next item on Rikki's agenda was to rehearse the pantomime *Sleeping Beauty* for the King's Theatre in Edinburgh with Wally Carr and Una MacLean. Before that I had to go to the Queen Mother's Hospital for a scan, and though Rikki wasn't able to take me in he said he would definitely be there to bring me home and we agreed that a couple of hours apart would give us both a rest from our endless search for names. We didn't want to know the sex of our offspring until he or she appeared, so we needed a boy's name as well as a girl's, and it was very time-consuming.

I took a taxi in to the hospital, reflecting how lucky I was to be a patient of a brilliant gynaecologist. The whole procedure of a maternity examination was something I knew nothing about but I was aware that a number of students had come into the room which I supposed was quite usual. Gradually it all became very quiet and soon only the nurses were left. For the first time I had a sense of foreboding and it was well-founded. The doctors came back, and they couldn't have been kinder, but I was totally unprepared for what they told me. The foetus was dead – it had never developed. Medically it's called a blighted ovum. There would be no baby.

All I could think about was how Rikki would feel. I had been building up his hopes and dreams and now they had come crashing down on us. I still felt in control of myself, and asked 'What happens now?' I was told to return to the hospital the next morning when they would operate, something they called a 'missed abortion'. That really stunned me, because when Rikki and I discovered how much we loved each other, I warned him that if he made me pregnant I would never have an abortion. Even with my lack of maternal instinct, the thought of destroying a child of Rikki's was beyond comprehension, and yet, here I was booking in to have it done in the morning. The irony of it didn't escape me.

I lay in the examination room thinking it all through, feeling grateful that at least I hadn't become hysterical; then Rikki walked in, and my self-control flew out of the window. To see his dear face looking so concerned made me cry my heart out and seconds later his arms were around me, and I dissolved in tears on his shoulder. He was so strong and comforting, as only he could be, and we were in our usual situation, which meant that whichever of us was upset, the other would have the strength for both of us. We went home with great sadness, but at least we were together and that made up for everything. To ask for more seemed selfish. We talked and talked and at last went to bed emotionally exhausted.

The next day Rikki had an early start for filming on location. I think it was *Rob Roy*, and we wouldn't meet again until the following evening, by which time I would be home, having had the unpleasant remains inside me removed. I drove to the hospital feeling as though my brain had become numb, and probably it had, for its own self-protection.

The operation was quick and straightforward, although I knew nothing about it. The first thing of which I was aware when I was back in my room regaining consciousness was not pain, but the most dreadful noise. Although we all had our own rooms most of the doors were open to the corridor, and someone there was sobbing at unreal decibels. I thought my head would split open with the din she was making, until I realised it was *me*! Self-control just doesn't seem to work under an anaesthetic.

The next problem was the walk along the corridor which I had been asked to do. Not that walking was at all difficult, but every room was occupied by a very new mother who had just had her baby. The whole area understandably was full of joy and celebration, but I felt it was insensitive to place patients who had just lost their dream alongside those who had achieved it. I might be quite wrong, perhaps it's to encourage the grieving process and acceptance of the situation, but it was like salt in a wound. That was many years ago and possibly things are much better now.

I drove home the next morning to be welcomed back by dear Mrs Wares who looked at me searchingly, and could probably tell by my face that it hadn't been the happiest of occasions. But all she said, in a gentle voice was, 'You take things awful sore,' and with that she packed me off to bed. I was only too happy to obey her instructions, and in no time was fast asleep. About two hours later I was wakened by the doorbell, and when Mrs Wares answered it there was quite a conversation going on, and when I heard the door shut curiosity got the better of me and I called her.

She came in looking rather puzzled, and when I asked her who had called, she explained it had been two men, who said they believed that a Katherine Fulton lived in this house, and when she said, 'Kate not Katherine,' they accepted that, and said they knew that she had just come home from the Queen Mother's Hospital. Mrs Wares agreed, but then they added that she had just had a baby. By this time Mrs Wares was suspicious and wanted to know who they were, why they had come to our house, and demanded identification from them. At that point one of the two who had not said one word until now, shouted, 'I told you it couldn't be this house, but would you listen?'

They sheepishly produced their identity cards. They were debt collectors.

I was glad they hadn't found the woman they were searching for. The thought of her happily returning home with her new baby, then being confronted by two bully boys, was just awful. It made me angry, and I wanted to find out what had been going on. Not that night, in the morning perhaps, but that evening we would drink a toast to each other's health, and accept that from now on there would be only Rikki and me. I was sure that in a very short time we would be so grateful that we had each other, the pain of loss we were feeling at the moment would ease, and as long as we were together we could cope with anything fate might have in store for us.

The moment Rikki came home that night I knew everything was going to be all right. Nothing in the world could be unhappy or frightening as long as he was there. We just naturally had our usual nightly talk, he told me about his day's filming, and I told him about the debt collectors. Rikki was livid, but I told him I was going to find out more about it in the morning, and in the meantime all I wanted was to go to bed and fall asleep in his arms, which I did.

Fortunately our physical time clocks were always on the same setting. We both hated getting up in the morning and were very gentle with each other, but this morning we wrapped each other in cotton wool! Even the dogs were quieter than usual. Isn't it amazing the way they can sense that something has happened?

Rikki drove off to his filming, looking less tense than he had been for some days, and then Mrs Wares arrived. It reminded me of the time, before I had come to live here, when Rikki told me that when Ethel left him and he was enjoying his bachelor days again, that he would often get home very late, round about four in the morning, and although he was so very tired he was also restless, and it wasn't until he heard Mrs Wares's key in the door that he would put his head on the pillow and fall into a deep and most peaceful sleep. Now I was the one getting the benefit of her reassuring presence, and how grateful I was for it.

Later in the morning I phoned the Queen Mother's Hospital and asked to speak to the Nursing Officer who was most helpful and understood why I wanted to know how the debt collectors had been given our address. She said she would make enquiries and phone me back. This she did after a very short time.

Apparently there had been a new girl on the reception desk who didn't know that addresses must never be disclosed, and the two men, who had been tipped off that the Katherine Fulton they were looking for could be found giving birth at the Queen Mother's, lost no time in finding out how to contact her. The nurse told them that she had just left that day, and was now at home. The men expressed great delight at that, and explained that she was a friend of theirs at work, they had brought her a large bouquet of flowers, but as they had missed her at the hospital was there any way the nurse could help them find her home address? Not realising she was being conned, the girl, trying to be helpful, gave them the hospital admissions book which had all the names and addresses of the patients. Fortunately for Katherine, they must have stopped at the first Kate Fulton they came across.

I'm not sure why, but I've always hoped they never found her. It was all so underhand and deceptive, but perhaps just a normal day's work for the two men. I suppose somebody has to do it.

By the time Rikki finished the television filming he went straight to the Lyceum Theatre. The opening night was to be introduced by Ludovic Kennedy, in the presence of HRH Princess Margaret, and it was fervently hoped that now the Lyceum would become Scotland's National Theatre. For some reason, which I could never fathom, the play chosen was *The Diary of a Scoundrel* by the nineteenth-century Russian dramatist Alexander Ostrovsky.

Two of the comedy roles were rather doddery aristocrats, played by Rikki and the delightful James Cairncross, who is a superb actor, and this was real type casting, getting a gentleman to play a gentleman – no one could have more impeccable manners than James. Of the two parts Rikki's was the more garbled, which Rikki loved, and he asked James if it would worry him if he were to change the content of his speeches each night. This was always a problem for his fellow actors who were used to sticking to the script and James looked less than enthusiastic. However, when Rikki promised that whatever he might say within his own speech, he would always come back to the script at the end of it and give the cue perfectly, James bravely agreed to give it a try.

It said a great deal for James that he was willing to take a gamble on such a prestigious opening night, but it worked, and Rikki thoroughly enjoyed himself. He was slightly taken aback when the company was presented to Princess Margaret, and she said to him, 'I'm told that you wrote your own part.' But for the rest of the run of the play Rikki greatly enjoyed being one half of a double act with James.

After that production was over we went as usual to Puerto de Pollensa, and it was so nice to see again the friends we had made, and seemed to continue to make; you could never be lonely in Pollensa! Katy's Bar was as busy as ever, and the buzz and the laughter made us so happy to be back. We met so many of our ex-pat friends who all seemed their usual cheerful selves, with the exception of David and Babs Short, who were very quiet, which wasn't at all like them.

After a most pleasant evening we were quite tired and having said 'good night' we set off for our hotel, but to our surprise, David and Babs said they would walk with us. We said we would be delighted to have their company, but surely it was rather out of their way? No, they said, we've moved. They had bought a flat in a new block right in the Port itself. This really was for Babs, who was a very keen artist and for some time had wanted a bigger apartment so that she could have a studio – and this new block had all the light she could ask for. It all seemed ideal, so what could be the problem? That turned out to be the fact that they hadn't sold their apartment at Katy's. They had been so anxious not to lose the flat they wanted that now they had the upkeep of two homes which was proving to be expensive, and although they had advertised their apartment, so far no one had shown any interest. By the time they had explained all this to us we had reached our hotel, but when we invited them in for a drink they didn't accept, and that wasn't like them. They clearly were worried about the situation they found themselves in. We tried to reassure them that the apartment had only been for sale for a very short time, and it was in a prime position, they were bound to sell it soon, and there would be no financial worries from then on.

We arranged to meet them at Katy's before lunch the next day, again wished them good night and hoped they would have a peaceful rest.

Our nocturnal chat was naturally about David and Babs. Rikki was rather non-committal about it all, but I was convinced that they would find a buyer soon. It was, after all, a good apartment. It had a good-sized sitting room, two bedrooms, a nice kitchen and bathroom, and although it had no sea view, it looked on to a *finka*, a Spanish farmhouse, and in this case it was a sheep farm with lovely green fields and hills, and the only noise that could be heard was in the evening, when the lovely sound of the bells around their necks announced that the sheep were coming home from their day in the hills. I could imagine that when you have spent the day in the heat of the sun, lying on the beach and swimming in the sea, returning from that to a green landscape with animals running free would be very relaxing.

After breakfast the next day we went as usual to the newsagent to see if they had any interesting books for sale. We still didn't buy the newspapers – we would catch up with the world when we got home. We were browsing through the shelves when David came in for his *Daily Telegraph,* so we went with him when he left, and the three of us sauntered in the sun along the pavement with the sea sparkling on our right. A typical Pollensa morning. Rikki and David were deep in conversation, so I was able to have a good look at the yachts which were in the harbour, but then their conversation caught my attention. Rikki asked David if the morning had brought any good news about their apartment, but David gloomily shook his head, then Rikki wanted to know if David had put the price up after it first went on the market, but he said, 'No, the price is still the same.' Rikki smiled, he took my hand and squeezed it hard, 'Right, David, I'll buy it.'

I couldn't believe what I was hearing. My husband, who loved his home so much that it was difficult to persuade him to go on holiday, was proposing to buy a permanent apartment abroad! I thought it wise to say absolutely nothing. Needless to say

David was overjoyed, and we agreed that when we met at lunchtime there would be plenty to talk about!

The moment Rikki and I were alone I asked him what on earth had persuaded him to buy the apartment. And he said that it was the first holiday we had shared, we both fell in love with Pollensa, and he felt we should own a tiny part of it. Now I understood, he was buying another 'home', but this one was for holidays!

The meeting at lunchtime was a very happy occasion. Babs was overjoyed that we were buying their apartment and so were we. We arranged that Rikki would pay for it before we left, but we couldn't move in until the Spring because Rikki had another commitment before then, putting on *Robinson Crusoe* at the King's in Glasgow, so it would be March before we could come back. David and Babs kindly said they would make sure it would be safe during the winter.

At the end of our holiday we flew home in a slightly bemused state, but it didn't last – preparing for the pantomime took care of that. I was always glad when the pantomime was at the King's in Glasgow because Rikki came home earlier at night and didn't have to leave so early in the day. In the cold wet winter nights, we would talk about what furniture and crockery we should send to Pollensa, and just thinking about it made us feel the sunshine!

The only real worry that year was my father's health. He was suffering a great deal of pain in his lower back and his doctor referred him to hospital. There they put him in traction, which for a man of his age and temperament did not go down well. He was not a willing patient but the staff looked after him with great kindness. When they took him off traction, which had done no good whatsoever, life was a little easier, but unfortunately his kidneys had been damaged.

I was concerned about leaving him to go to Pollensa, but the hospital assured me he would be all right, as indeed he was. I sent him a postcard from there every day, and told him we had bought our apartment. As soon as we got home I went straight to see him, and found he had changed a lot. He was much calmer and seemed to be more contented. When I arrived I went to find the charge nurse to ask if I could be allowed to give Daddy the champagne I had brought for him. He didn't reply at first, so I said if it might upset the medication he was being given, then of course I would take it away. At that he shook his head and said, 'I'm sorry, I had to think for a moment, of course you can give him champagne, but he has just had his whisky, so it would be better to give it to him at the end of your visit.'

It was wonderful to see Daddy out of pain, and he said happily, 'Do you know where I am?' I confessed that I didn't, so he said 'I'm in a cave in Pollensa, I can hear the sea and it's lovely and cool, but best of all, there's a table the whole length of the cave and it's covered with bottles of every spirit and wine you've ever heard of, and it's all mine.' I could only think that whatever they were giving my father with his whisky, it was certainly doing the trick. I think it was called a Brompton cocktail, and was certainly greatly appreciated by this particular patient!

Rikki was extremely kind to Bill, my father, and visited him regularly, as did my sister Doreen and her husband, but Rikki had a problem with shopping for Bill because he insisted that Rikki should buy cigarettes for him. We had now been told that Daddy was dying of lung cancer, so cigarettes were strictly forbidden, and Rikki would face an irate father-in-law when he came back without them. I felt it was bolting the stable door after the horse had gone – would the solace of a cigarette have made any difference to the inevitable death? Perhaps I'm wrong about that, but at the time it just seemed heartless.

One morning I had a phone call from the hospital to say that Daddy's condition had worsened and they suggested that I should go straight there. This of course I did, but how I wished Rikki was at home and not working that day. When I saw my father I was sure he was unconscious, but the nurse told me he was still aware of some things and could certainly hear anything I said to him. He looked awful, his face was often contorted with pain, and his hands clawed endlessly at the blanket covering him. I tried everything I could think of to soothe him. I spoke to him softly, wiped his brow with a cool cloth, and tried to calm his frenetic hands, but nothing worked, and I realised that he and I were on different planets and we could no longer communicate.

There was no point in staying. It would be better to go home and look after my mother who was staying with us. I was so very glad she had decided not to go to the hospital with me. It would have been dreadful to see her Bill like that, and he wouldn't have known she was there.

I made us a light lunch, and she was marvellous. I suppose she had been preparing herself for this day, but instead of being mournful, all she wanted to talk about were the good times, and there were plenty of those. I learned more about my parents that afternoon than I would have believed possible, and it was so good for us both. My loss was heartfelt, but it couldn't begin to compare with hers, and yet here we were, reliving happiness.

Rikki came home and we were so glad to see him, he was so understanding and sympathetic, and while I went into the kitchen to make our evening meal, Rikki took Mummy into the drawing room for a well-deserved drink before dinner. The day before I had made a steak and kidney pie, so tonight it just had to be heated and all the vegetables were ready, but before I could take them through the phone rang. It was a senior nurse from the hospital to tell me that Daddy had just died. I thanked him for telling me and put down the phone. I sat there for some time with a thousand thoughts about him going through my head, then I realised that I had to make a decision, should I tell Mummy now or let her enjoy her reminiscences? I chose the latter. I would break the news to her when we talked after dinner. I picked up some dishes to carry them through to the dining room when Mummy appeared in the kitchen. 'Who was that on the phone?' she asked, and before I could reply she said, 'It was the hospital, wasn't it?' I nodded.

'What did they . . . say?'

I took a deep breath. 'Daddy died ten minutes ago, I'm so very sorry.'

She was amazing. All she said was, 'Thank heavens, that's an end to the pain he was in. Can I carry some of these plates through for you?' She was made of stern stuff, my mother!

15

HAIL TO THEE, BLITHE SPIRIT

The next day Rikki and I went into town to see Wyllie and Lochhead, the undertakers. They were most polite, and suitably solemn. After I had signed all the necessary documents I was asked if I would like to see my father. This took me by surprise. I knew that he had been brought to their 'Rooms of Rest', but hadn't realised that I could see him. I thanked them, but said that at the moment I wasn't sure, but I would let them know. With that we drove home to my mother.

I obviously had a lot to learn, I'd never dealt with a funeral before, and neither had Rikki. He had been away when each of his parents died, and I imagine it would be his eldest brother John who arranged their burials. Wyllie and Lochhead were clearly going to be helpful and the following day when we found we needed to order more cars, I told Rikki that I would go to their place in Pitt Street rather than phone them. He almost certainly guessed why. I had spent the night thinking about Daddy, and did I really want to see him one last time? The answer was a resounding 'yes'. To see him at peace, instead of the painful picture I last had of him, would be comforting.

Arriving at Pitt Street I was put in the care of a most kindly man, with a rather odd name for an undertaker, a Mr Smiley. We got the cars sorted out, and then I said that having thought it over, I would like to say goodbye to my father. Mr Smiley was very approving and told me that 'our Mr Johnson' would take me there. He made a quick phone call, and in moments there was a knock at the door. It seemed that I was not destined to meet 'our Mr Johnson' just yet, as he and Mr Smiley had a lengthy conversation in the corridor, followed by a number of doors being opened and closed. Shortly afterwards a rather flushed Mr Smiley came in saying hopefully, 'Have you any shopping to do, Mrs Fulton?' On learning that I had not, he went rather wearily to the door apologising for the delay, and assuring me that he would be back very shortly.

Then there was trouble! The 'rooms' were just like old-fashioned train compartments, with the same sliding doors, all adjoining, and forming a square. Every door was opened and slammed noisily back, while the voices became more and more vociferous. I so wanted to go out and see what was going on, but I knew I could only make matters worse.

At long last Mr Smiley, wearing a very brave face, returned to tell me that 'our Mr Johnson' would be with us in two minutes.

I had to say to him, 'Mr Smiley, you can't just leave it at that; you have to tell me what has been going on.'

He swallowed hard, and said, 'I'm very sorry, I'm afraid we lost father, we were looking for a Mr Fulton, not a Mr Craig-Brown.'

I couldn't control myself, and hooted with laughter. Not being prepared to tell him what I found so funny, I composed myself for the arrival of 'our Mr Johnson'.

Like many families we have a family catchphrase. Ours came from a Glasgow Fair Friday many years ago. We went every summer to Kyles Hydro, just outside Rothesay, which meant getting the train from Central Station before boarding the wonderful *Waverley* to go 'doon the watter'. One year we arrived early and had to wait a bit for the train, which we didn't mind at all, as there was so much going on in the area leading to the platforms. We were amazed at a most unlikely couple. He was about six feet three in height and well over 20 stone in weight. She was tiny, barely five feet and very thin. Despite this, he was hanging on to her arm to keep himself upright, and it was clear he had started to celebrate the Fair very early in the morning, if not the night before, and all he could say to his wife, over and over again was, 'Don't you lose me.' She looked as though nothing would give her more pleasure, but loyally guided him to their train, and thus was born our family catchphrase.

I can't remember a time when we were crossing a road when Daddy wouldn't take my arm and say, 'Don't you lose me.'

Now when I was alone in his 'Room' I had to say to him, 'Oh Daddy, they *did*.'

I was glad I had gone to say goodbye to him. He certainly looked peaceful, though that was in spite of the heavy make-up that had been given to him. With the red lips and rouged cheeks he looked as if he was about to appear in comic opera, but then as he had spent his life longing to be a comedian perhaps it wasn't too inappropriate! Those few moments alone with him remain precious.

Of course when I got home I couldn't wait to tell Rikki about the chaos Daddy and I had caused. It was a beautiful day so we went into the back garden because I wanted to be sure that Mummy didn't hear what I was saying, thinking that it wouldn't amuse her as it had me. Within minutes Rikki and I were in each other's arms, laughing, but we stopped when we heard Mummy knocking on the guest-room window.

We waved up to her, and then worried! Sure enough, she came into the garden minutes later, wanting to know what on earth we were laughing at. We tried to hedge round it, but she would have none of it. I said it was something I had been telling Rikki which was private. That she would not accept; according to Mummy anything I said to Rikki I could say to her. But it might upset you I protested. 'Let me be the judge of that,' she said firmly, and so I told her of the time I had had with Mr

Smiley and 'our Mr Johnson'. She listened silently, and then gave a shriek of laughter. I'm sure Daddy would have been pleased to hear her.

His funeral was very straightforward, and Mummy couldn't have shown more dignity than she did that day. After the service everyone came back to our house for what is politely called 'refreshments', but there was plenty to eat as well. Mummy had made up her mind that she would go home that night. 'I have to learn to live on my own,' she said. Thankfully a friend and neighbour for many years, Anne Thompson, also a widow, was going to stay with her as long as she felt she could help. Isn't it remarkable how in times of crisis there always seems to be someone who is prepared to come to the rescue?

Now that Rikki and I were on our own again there was a lot to be done. He had been asked to play *The Miser* by Molière, on television. This he was happy to do – he really loved being in his plays – and Molière translates perfectly into Scots. I sometimes wondered if there was some kind of affinity between them. They were both writers, directors and comedy actors, and they were both searching for laughter. Fortunately *The Miser* was filmed at the BBC in Glasgow.

Shortly after Rikki had finished the filming, he had a phone call from the wonderful Joan Knight, from Perth Theatre. She wanted both Rikki and me to play the leads in Noel Coward's *Blithe Spirit*. I felt as though I was living in a dream world. I had played Elvira twice, and loved the part, but would Rikki agree to play the Noel Coward role? He did! I'm sure it was only because Joan was to be our director that he accepted, as we both had such admiration and affection for her.

I looked forward to the production in a way I had never done before, and it was every bit as wonderful as I had hoped. To make things even better Mummy phoned to say that friends were going to bring her to Perth during our first week in production, and that really pleased me because I had been worried about her health. She seemed to be a bit off-colour, but if she could face the journey to us she must be feeling better. Rehearsals with Joan were a dream, and full of laughter. I could hardly believe what was happening: here I was, not only spending all day and night with Rikki, but working with him as well!

I was in seventh heaven, but I don't want to give the wrong impression. We weren't living in a fool's paradise and sometimes used to have the most flaming rows!

Needless to say I was the cause of the first one. I had been watching a very old repeat of *Steptoe and Son* which I enjoyed, but when Rikki, who had never liked the series, came into the room he said he didn't know how I could watch it – they should let sleeping dogs lie, and not try to bring back comedians who had had their day. How then, I asked him, could he justify bringing back Francie and Josie? He glared at me, didn't say a word, stormed out of the room, picked up his car keys from the hall sideboard, and strode to the garage. A moment later the Mercedes went down the drive like a dose of Epsom salts, turned into the road and disappeared over the hill in a cloud of dust.

Realising that I might just have annoyed him a little (!), I wasn't sure what to do. I couldn't possibly run after him, and if I took my car out how could I discover where he had gone? I thought about this deeply for two minutes, and then went to bed. There Rikki found me, fast asleep, when he returned at 4am. He had driven over the brow of the hill, just out of sight, and had been waiting for me to come looking for him.

I always thought our rows were over fairly quickly, but an actor friend told me that one lasted for three days when we were doing a play in Aberdeen. Apparently the entire cast gathered in the wings to watch us play the love scenes through gritted teeth!

Playing in *Blithe Spirit* was something I will never forget. A lovely and talented actress, Anne Kidd, was cast as Ruth who was the living wife, while Elvira was the ghost of the first wife, dressed in grey chiffon, with long grey hair and completely grey skin. I remember my brother-in-law, Tom, came looking for me one afternoon during a matinée, and he was told he would find me in the wings. When he arrived I had my back to him, and on turning round I was very afraid he was having a heart attack. He became greyer than Elvira. No one had told him he was looking for a ghost!

Mummy came to see the play during the first week, and thankfully enjoyed it. So much so that she said she was looking forward to seeing it again when we came to Glasgow. We had a few free weeks before we opened at the King's, and thank goodness we had. When we came home from Perth I was again worried about her health and her doctor asked me to take her to hospital for tests saying he would phone me when he was given the results. This he did, and it was very bad news indeed. Mummy had to be taken to the Victoria Infirmary; they had discovered terminal cancer. Naturally she hated the idea of going into hospital, and wanted to know why she had to go. It wasn't possible to tell her the truth, so I said they wanted to do some more tests. Her reply was, 'Well, they had better be quick because you open at the King's soon and I'm going to be there on the first night.' I took her a poster advertising us in *Blithe Spirit*, and she put it on the wall opposite her bed in her room so she would remember the date she was determined to keep.

Sadly it was not to be. She developed a secondary cancer, and that was the cause of her death. Thankfully for her, it was quick. I went to see her every day, but she was most unhappy in the Victoria, and although she had her own room the door was kept open and she hated the lack of privacy. One afternoon when I arrived, she was sleeping very peacefully, and I said to the nurse who was there, 'It seems a shame to wake her,' and she replied softly, 'You won't be able to.' That was the last time I saw the woman I had loved all my life. I could only be grateful that her death was so peaceful, and thanks to the hospital staff, pain-free.

It was quite different from the way Daddy had died, and I was able to remember how calm and lovely she looked, which was a solace.

It was a quiet funeral, although many neighbours and all her bridge friends bade her farewell. I could only be glad that she had so enjoyed seeing our play in Perth because obviously she couldn't keep her promise to be at our first night in Glasgow.

I was always more nervous playing in Glasgow than anywhere else. Needless to say it didn't affect Rikki at all. He never knew what 'first-night nerves' were, he just couldn't wait to get on to that stage and make people laugh.

Our opening night brought Rikki and me quite a surprise. If you've ever seen *Blithe Spirit*, you'll know that in the final scene everything falls off the walls and the mantelpiece, so rather ancient pictures and ornaments are used so that nothing of value will be broken. One thing which was attractive was a carriage clock that had lain in the prop room for years and had never worked. It now sat in the centre of the mantelpiece.

The first act of the play includes a séance presided over by Madame Arcati, famously played by Margaret Rutherford in the film, and this conjures up the ghost of Elvira. The dress rehearsal went smoothly in the afternoon and all seemed to be well. I couldn't help thinking of Mummy, and how she had wanted to be there that night, and I knew Rikki was feeling the same. Only moments after the curtain rose that night we could tell they were going to be a lovely audience. I was listening to the cast onstage through the tannoy in my dressing room, waiting to make my entrance. It was very clear, and I could hear every word. What I couldn't work out was a strange rather pretty tinkling sound which came in at regular intervals.

I made my entrance as Elvira and discovered from where the noise was coming. It was the little clock on the mantelpiece, chiming with regularity every few minutes. There is a belief that when someone dies, a clock stops. My mother was renowned as being very contrary, and I thought it would be just like her, instead of stopping a clock, she would start one!

The moment the curtain fell at the end of the first act, I went straight to Rikki who was already heading in my direction, we looked at each other, and simultaneously said, 'She's here.' Mummy always kept her promises, and she said she would be there on our fist night, and she was! We both said, 'Welcome, Nita,' but the stage management didn't share our enthusiasm. They could not stop the clock from chiming. At last they gave up, opened the clock and removed all the works inside. The empty clock sat silently on the mantelpiece from then on. It is said that every theatre has a ghost but I wouldn't be surprised if the King's now has two, the new one being Nita, Rikki Fulton's mother-in-law!

That winter saw us in Inverness for pantomime, *Cinderella*, directed by one of our good friends, Clive Perry. I suppose that as I was, of course with Rikki, they decided I should be put to work, so I was cast as the Fairy Godmother, an experience I will never forget. It was being presented traditionally, which means the Godmother appears first, with a monologue before the Pantomime starts. I remember my first lines were something like, 'From the glades of fairyland, swift was my flight.' That was bad enough, but what made it worse was that the costume they had made for my size ten made me look as though I weighed about 20 stone and that even a shipbuilding crane wouldn't get me off the ground, far less fly.

That was annoying but not all that important, except I did feel sorry for my aunt and uncle, Ian and Mabel Cameron, who were very well known in Inverness; but if they were sensible they probably disowned me!

All was not lost, because Rikki and Walter Carr were very popular and had the audiences roaring with laughter, and that's what it was all about after all.

We were also wonderfully lucky to have rented a villa in

Darris Road, Lochardle. There we had the best neighbours anyone could wish for, and we still exchange Christmas cards. On our right lived Mr and Mrs Ross, who were delightful, and on our left, Mr and Mrs Kennedy. The whole neighbourhood was friendly, though I'm sure they found it somewhat eccentric that we walked our dogs around their roads after midnight, but they just accepted it. That year was bitterly cold. It was 1978 and I will never forget a washing I put out one night before we went to bed. In the back garden there was one of those circular clothes lines, the ones that look like parasols without a top, and around the outer edge I had hung a lot of my tights, in various colours. The next morning they were frozen solid, and I promise you nothing looks so laughably absurd as frozen tights. Even the dogs were laughing!

We had our farewell company party on the Friday night as most theatre companies do because on the final night, the Saturday, everyone is busy getting their dressing rooms cleared, and the stage management are taking down the sets – it's usually pandemonium.

Driving back to Darris Road, we decided to take the dogs for their walk before we had supper, and because it was so cold I took off a very large topaz ring Rikki had given me so that I could get my gloves on. I put it in the pocket of the fur coat I was wearing. The icy weather gave us all an appetite and when we got back to the house I made a large supper for all four of us.

The next night was our last and we hoped the roads would not be a problem in the morning when driving home. We had taken both our cars to Inverness because you need a lot of luggage when you're going to be away for months in the winter. Rikki took practically all of it, I took what was left and most importantly, the dogs.

On Sunday morning we loaded up the cars. Rikki put all the cases and boxes in either the boot or the back seat of his, and then threw our coats on top of them inside the car. In mine, we put all the bits and pieces in the boot so we could leave the back seat free for the dogs' rug, and of course Jeeves and Jonathon. They happily jumped in and we were off! Rikki naturally led the way and I followed. It seemed as though it was going to be trouble-free, and it wasn't even snowing. I began to find it relaxing, the road wasn't very busy, and the countryside and the hills covered in snow were beautiful, and looked so calm and peaceful. I knew Rikki would be enjoying it too, and his car would be filled with his favourite music. What a lovely way to drive home.

The enjoyment was short-lived, and as we approached Kingussie the police were turning all drivers back. The road south was completely blocked and the only alternative was to go to the east coast, to Aberdeen and then south. Rikki and I were determined to get home as soon as possible so we headed for Aberdeen. The first half hour was fine, then the snow started, but it wasn't just snow, it was a blizzard, and we realised how the roads had become blocked. I had never been in a blizzard before, and found it quite startling. I had always thought that snow came straight down from the sky, but in these conditions it came horizontally, sweeping across the hedges and lying on the verges, narrowing the traffic lanes to two instead of four. Now we were in single file, and I was so grateful it was Rikki leading the convoy, and not me.

To make matters worse, in the bitter cold my windscreen washer froze. I couldn't clean the windscreen and it was now getting dark so that all the cars coming from the opposite direction had their headlights on and they were blinding. The thing that worried me was that the dogs would sense my panic and react to it. If they did, they showed no sign of it, and never let out a bark or even a yelp. I was so grateful to them because I personally felt like barking my head off. I tried to follow their example of self-restraint but it wasn't easy. I felt trapped, I couldn't see properly through the windscreen and there was no way I could stop on a single-lane road as it would have meant the long tailback of cars would have had to stop also, and I don't think they would have been too pleased.

We drove for hours – it's quite a long way from Kingussie to Aberdeen – and by the time we reached the outskirts at Dyce I was praying that Rikki would stop. He did! There was a Post House hotel on our side of the road and he swung into it, closely followed by someone who, as he discovered on opening my car door, was a juddering wreck!

We were bundled into the hotel, and knew no more until breakfast. We then had to take a circuitous route back because of blocked roads and were more than happy to arrive in Glasgow.

It took us a leisurely time to unpack all our luggage for the winter, and it wasn't until a week later that I realised I hadn't found my topaz ring. We tried to remember when we had last seen it, and of course realised it was on that cold night when I had put it in my coat pocket. I phoned the hotel in case it might have fallen out there, but it hadn't been found, so I called our kind neighbours, the Rosses, in case it had fallen on the pebble drive. They told us there was still snow lying but they would look in the morning. They phoned the next day to tell us there was no sign of it.

I hate losing things, but especially a present given to me by Rikki.

Some weeks later we were invited up to Tain by the people who were running the oil rig at Nigg. They were planning a dinner followed by entertainment, and Rikki was asked to compère and provide the comedy. This he did, and it was a wonderful evening. The Alexander Brothers were there, and Tom and Jack are always the best of company. Later I was chatting with our host, and he asked about our stay in Inverness. I told him we had enjoyed it, but for me it had been spoiled by the loss of my ring. He asked where it might be, and I told him I was sure it must have dropped on the drive when our coats were thrown on the back seat of the car.

'We'll find it for you,' he said.

I looked at him in astonishment, and he explained that they would send down a metal detector by one of their helicopters and sweep the drive with it. I protested that they shouldn't think of wasting so much time, but they were adamant, and a few days later we had a phone call at home to say they had carried out 'Operation Topaz', and the ring was certainly not in the drive of the house. That was disappointing, but how very kind of them to have looked for it, and now we would have to accept the ring had gone.

The bitter winter at last ended, to be followed by a bright spring, and everyone felt the better for it. It made such a change to see sunshine again, and the verdant leaves on the trees. One Sunday, walking back to Darris Road, Mrs Ross suggested to her husband that they have one last look in the drive of number 16. Without much hope they went on to the pebble drive, and within seconds she saw something sparkling among the stones. The topaz! There wasn't a mark or scratch on it, the covering of snow had protected it all winter. I can never thank them enough for finding it, and sending it back to me. It's now an even more special piece of jewellery to me.

Rikki did a lot of filming that year, including an excellent part in an episode of *Bergerac* with John Nettles, playing a Scots comedian doing a summer season in Jersey. Filming for that was difficult because of the weather – there was only one day in the whole fortnight when the sun came out, and then it was only for an hour. We liked Jersey very much, especially the choice we had of so many excellent restaurants.

It seemed no time at all before we had to go home to prepare for Rikki's pantomime, but this year we were not looking forward to it. Rikki was to be in Plymouth with Harry Worth, Sam Kelly and Ian Lavender. We liked the sound of the cast list, but it was so far away, and meant we would miss Christmas and Hogmanay at home. We were both sorry about that, and then I thought, why should we be dictated to by the calendar – what was wrong with celebrating Hogmanay in August?

We invited everyone that we would have done on the 31st of December, and I started to put up the Christmas decorations. I think I gave our paperboy the fright of his life. He was new to delivering papers, and he probably had never seen a truly demented woman before. What else could he think? He saw through the glass front door a female in a dressing gown wearing yellow rubber gloves, putting fairy lights on a decorated Christmas tree in August.

Our guests were splendid. They all came 'first footing', complete with bits of coal, silver coins and pieces of bread. It was simply the best Hogmanay party we ever gave and it was broad daylight when people began to think of going home. I was told some days later that a couple who lived further down our road, whom we didn't know, were driving home after someone else's party and passed our house at dawn. Nothing was said, but later at breakfast she said, 'You're not going to believe what I thought I saw last night . . .' Before she could say another word, he cut in with, 'Oh thank God, I thought it was just me.'

Plymouth was not pleasant. We liked the cast, all of them, and particularly Sam Kelly, and it's so good to see he's such a success. We liked the town, we had such a nice flat (it was modern with what was virtually a glass wall looking over the water, with Cornwall on the other side), but and it was a big *but*, Rikki had forgotten how much he hated doing English pantomimes.

It was also extremely hard work and by the Sunday he was always exhausted. Unfortunately, one week his London agent, Richard Stone, phoned to make an appointment for him to meet a casting director about a film. Rikki had a matinée that day, so I took the call and noted the date for the next Sunday.

I promised to pass on the message, but assured Richard that Rikki would refuse to go. Which was just what he did. 'Go to

London on my only free day,' he roared. I took that to be a 'no'.

Then the daily phone calls from the agency began. Sometimes it was one of the very nice girls who now run the agency and who were being so kind, but were determined that Rikki should not pass up this opportunity.

The film was to be *Gorky Park*, taken from the novel by Martin Cruz Smith, with the screen adaptation by Dennis Potter.

'You must get him there on Sunday, it's the film director himself who wants to meet him,' I was ordered.

Somehow or other we were on the train going to Elstree, and Rikki was in the most foul mood. I had bought and read the book, which I had with me, but he absolutely refused to look at it. That was a relief, I knew the part they were thinking of for him was the head of the KGB and the description of him in the book was less than flattering. Amongst other flaws, his arms being so long he looked like a gorilla! The less Rikki knew about that the better.

The director was Michael Apted and he was charming. He asked Rikki if he had read the book. 'No,' he snapped, 'tell me about it.' Rather taken aback, Michael outlined the story and the character, but he was very ill at ease because Rikki's eyes never left his face. After about five minutes of this Michael gave in and addressed the end of the book to the carpet. Having finished, he thanked Rikki for coming to London, and began the usual speech, 'Of course we'll be in touch with you soon.' But Rikki would have none of it, 'Do you want me to play this part, or not?'

Michael said rather hoarsely, 'Yes, I do,' and said he would contact Richard Stone in the morning. With that we left. No wonder the poor man had felt uncomfortable. He told someone later that Rikki had the most evil eyes he had ever seen, but considering Rikki had been playing a member of the KGB from the moment he arrived at the studio, that wasn't surprising!

We had a much more sociable evening when Michael came to

supper after seeing *Cinderella*, though how he could reconcile a pantomime dame with the KGB I don't know.

They couldn't get permission to film in Russia, so it was made in Finland, in Helsinki, and a few days in Stockholm. There had been a discussion as to whether it would be better to film in Austria or Finland, and it was decided that the necessary snow would be more safely found in Finland. Sure enough on the first day's filming the field they were using was deep in snow. The following morning it had gone, and never came back. They had to have the local fire brigade spray foam over all the fields while Austria hid under a blanket of snow.

That was the first problem, and many others followed, the final one being the pine martens; they should have been sables but they weren't allowed out of Russia. The last shot of the film has to be the sables escaping and scampering to freedom. The sables/martens had to be taken care of, and they were. Their cages were kept warm and they had plenty of food and water, with the result of course that when their cages were opened for the big escape, they raised sleepy heads and said, we're not going out there, it's much too cosy in here. It took a lot of persuasion and rattling of cages to make them move at all.

We greatly enjoyed meeting the other people involved in the film. There was only one other couple there, Ian Bannen with his lovely wife Marilyn and we often dined together and so enjoyed their company. The four of us were all lovers of pets, so while our men were working, Marilyn and I would be feeding the ducks. I've never seen so many. There was a large expanse of grass in front of the hotel and at night you couldn't see a blade of it – it was completely covered with ducks, hundreds of them.

Rikki and I were dreadfully sad when Ian died; they had been such a loving and perfect couple. The phrase Rikki used when two people deeply in love were separated by death, was 'the cruel wrenching apart,' and we felt that for Marilyn.

There were so many people we liked on the set, and Rikki and Lee Marvin in particular enjoyed each other's company. They would sit together in their named chairs, discussing the younger members of the cast, looking for all the world like a scene out of Chekhov. The only one they couldn't come to terms with was William Hurt, who played the lead in *Gorky Park*. He is an intense actor, who most mornings would sit in the middle of a field concentrating on his part. That was fine, but if anyone dared to call 'good morning' to him, his contemplation would be ruined for the day, as was most of his filming. Mr Marvin and Mr Fulton found this impossible to understand. They were of the old school, whose axiom was 'remember the lines and don't trip over the furniture'.

We were on location for a number of weeks, and although the work was quite different, the relaxation at the end of the day was just the same as in the theatre. Most of us were staying at the Intercontinental Hotel, and everyone would gather in the lounge to have a drink and discuss the day they had had. It was all very civilised and enjoyable, and I remember Michael Elphick being so funny and entertaining. Someone who never joined the party was the writer Dennis Potter, who was the victim of a crippling illness but in spite of that sometimes wrote magnificently. It was a pity he disliked Rikki so much.

The reason for this was a suggestion Rikki had made about changing the end of the film, one that Michael Apted liked very much, and he asked Dennis Potter to write Rikki's version instead of the one, he, Dennis had written. Naturally that did not go down well with Mr Potter, and he became unspeakably rude to us. In a full dining room in the hotel he would talk at the top of his voice, so everyone could hear, about how much he disliked the Scots, particularly any of them involved in his film. At first we argued with him, but then we ignored him, and that made him angrier than ever. Some time later I read in his autobiography that he deliberately set out to annoy and upset people. It made him feel better. A strange twisted mind, but a sensational writer.

16

SUPERCOP AT THE GENERAL ASSEMBLY

After our cold but snowless spring in Helsinki, even Rikki was longing for some sunshine, and we decided to go to Majorca to thaw out. We were enjoying our apartment there tremendously, and every time we went we added a little more to the comfort of it. Entertaining was bliss, the custom among the ex-pats being that if you were invited for drinks, that's exactly what you got; if you opened a packet of crisps, it was a party! They had a strict code of practice, and rounds of drinks were carefully monitored. One gentleman in particular complained bitterly if someone ordered a gin and tonic, maintaining that this was two drinks, and the culprit should stand the next two rounds. We were in a very happy position for drinks parties, for if anyone ordered anything out of the ordinary it took 80 seconds to get to Katy's Bar and collect whatever had been requested. We had a happy and restful holiday, and Rikki returned home refreshed for pantomime, which thankfully was in Edinburgh that winter.

Before the pantomime ended Richard phoned to say that the playwright Michael Frayne wanted Rikki to star in a new production he was putting on at the Greenwich Theatre, London, with George Cole as co-star. When Rikki was sent the script he thought it had potential. Finding somewhere to stay was the problem.

We now had only one dog as the ever-popular Jonathon had died of heart failure; it seems he had had a heart murmur. We were afraid that Jeeves would pine for him, but although he was in the room when Jonathon died, he didn't even turn round. Suddenly he was like a puppy again, and we realised that for ten years he had been jealous of his brother, and had now come into his own! Rikki was so sad at Jonathon's death. I will never forget when our loved little dog had been taken away, returning to the bedroom to find Rikki on the floor rubbing at a tiny blood stain with a handkerchief which was soaked with his tears.

Moving to London for some months would take a bit of organising; hotels for that length of time would be enormously expensive, and more importantly, would they accept Jeeves? Suddenly I had an idea, 'Why don't we buy a flat there?'

Rikki thought I was totally mad, but he later conceded it wasn't a bad idea. We would be quite independent, and we could have Jeeves with us.

Now we were searching the papers for a small place to live. We found it! It was only a studio apartment, but it was right at Marble Arch, and it had an underground car park. We went down to see it, buy it and furnish it, all in three days. We arrived with sleeping bags for the first night, which would have to be spent on the floor, only to discover that they hadn't quite finished painting the apartment. They promised to finish within two hours, so we went for coffee, and then bought a television set so we could watch the news, especially anything to do with Scotland.

I can't say we had a very comfortable night, and were glad to get up the next morning to go shopping. It was all furniture shopping, and even in Harrods I didn't go near the fashion department. We had to buy a sofa bed because the sitting room, the only room, was too small for a bed and a sofa. It really was like a large hotel room with its own bathroom and kitchen, but it was all we needed.

Rikki started to rehearse at Greenwich; the cast was excellent, especially George Cole, but then he always is. The play was called *Liberty Hall*, and this was a second shot at it. Originally it had been produced under another title, but Michael Frayne had rewritten it. Rikki's part needed a great deal of comedy business added to it, which of course Rikki was only too happy to supply. But he had a bit of a problem with the director, Alan Dosser, who, though he accepted all the ad-lib comedy that was being put in, was not enthusiastic about it – unlike Michael Frayne who went in practically every night to see what Rikki was up to, and loved it.

The audiences also, even more importantly, enjoyed it. Then word went round that the mighty Michael Codron was coming in the following night to book it for London's West End. The company were highly delighted, and the next night just before the curtain went up Alan Dosser gave a talk to the company, wishing them well, but to Rikki he said, 'I want my production back. I want Michael Codron to see my work, not yours.'

Rikki accepted this, and promised he would do exactly what his director asked for. He did. With the result that the first act passed very quickly. There were no laughs.

At the interval Alan Dosser came to the men's dressing room and asked Rikki what he was doing. To which Rikki could only reply, 'You asked for your production back, now you've got it.'

Michael Codron was not impressed, and the play did not go to the West End. Some time later Walter Carr played the same part in Scotland, and said despairingly to Rikki that he had been told the play was full of laughs, but he couldn't find a single one!

Before the Greenwich season ended Rikki was asked to play Autolycus in Jonathan Miller's production of Shakespeare's *The Winter's Tale*, for the BBC. He was highly delighted to be in such a prestigious production, even though it meant a much longer stay in London. We were so glad now to have bought our little apartment.

Rikki had played in quite a few Shakespearian productions, but Autolycus presented difficulties. He was a rogue and vagabond and Rikki couldn't decide which accent he should use, because it was thought that he would play it in Scots but he didn't want to do that. How could the Scots possibly be called 'rogues and vagabonds'? We talked about it for hours, until I suggested that if Shakespeare had given him a first name, he could have been Seamus O'Tolycus. Rikki liked the idea and played it with an Irish accent. He was greatly pleased when later he was sent a book on Shakespeare which was given to schools, describing him as the 'definitive' Autolycus.

I have to confess our long stay in London was rather challenging. Rikki was away all day and night. Mornings at the BBC and evenings at Greenwich. Dear Jeeves was a problem too. He hated to be left alone, but of course wasn't allowed in food shops, and as the fridge had to be small to fit the kitchen, I had to buy small quantities of food at a time, and when I got back Jeeves immediately demanded to be taken for a walk. He thought Hyde Park was his back garden, and was most annoyed when guns were fired there for the Queen's birthday. She might have warned him! I seemed to spend each day going in and out, either shopping or taking Jeeves out. Our top-hatted doorman must have wondered just what I was up to . . .

After all the time we had been away, going home to Glasgow was a dream. Suddenly we had a house with masses of space to put things, freezers to fill, and a back and front garden for Jeeves. Rikki was one happy man! Home meant so much to him.

He worried a lot about our now owning three homes. One day I found him looking extremely troubled, and asked what was wrong. He looked at me, beseeching an answer, and said, 'It was all right when we only had this house, but now we have three I don't know in which one to have my last illness.'

I decided that was certainly a problem only he could solve!

Rikki's next project was something different. Being a devout follower of Molière he wanted to do a Scottish version of *Le Bourgeois Gentilhomme*. This could only be achieved with the help of . . . well, how can I describe Denise Coffey? Wonderful, brilliant etc. are inadequate – perhaps the only word is unique! She made a name for herself playing comedy in films, and then was sought-after for radio programmes because of her wit.

She came to stay with us while she translated the Molière into English, and then Rikki translated it into Scots. It was a joy to have her in our home and the three of us could have talked and laughed for years! We didn't have that luxury, as the new production, now with the title *A Wee Touch O' Class*, had been booked for the Edinburgh Festival in 1985.

The play was booked into the Churchill Theatre, which they enjoyed playing, but it was too small for all the audiences who wanted to see it. Edinburgh's answer was to invite them back the following year to a larger theatre.

After the Festival Rikki was straight into recording for *Scotch and Wry*, a series that had really taken off. It had all come about thanks to Gordon Menzies. He was Head of Education programmes, but one day he marched upstairs to the Head of Light Entertainment and announced he would like to do a comedy series with Rikki Fulton. They agreed to try it, and Rikki had the time of his life. He loved everything about it – the script writers, and his fellow actors Gregor Fisher, Tony Roper, Gerard Kelly, and the amazing Claire Nielson, who could play any part from a sex symbol to a hag! Rikki's most popular characters were the gloomy Rev. I.M. Jolly and the very dim Supercop. The series ran for quite a time, and then became an extremely popular show at Hogmanay. What with that, and pantomime, Rikki was kept happily busy.

One summer we had a most unusual invitation. It was to spend a day and night at the Palace of Holyrood in Edinburgh during the General Assembly of the Church of Scotland. The Queen was represented by the Lord High Commissioner, who for a second term of office was Lord MacFarlane of Bearsden.

I had been warned what to expect. A friend told me that our cases would be unpacked for us by a housekeeper (a good excuse to buy some lacy lingerie), and that we would have separate bedrooms. When Dinner Dress was worn, the lady's evening gown should touch the floor, no ballet-length nonsense! It was certainly going to be an experience. We were sent a letter telling us what time we should arrive, and, most importantly, a Police Pass, which we would need to get through the gates of the Palace.

On the day we set off after lunch, and had a leisurely drive through to Edinburgh. As we were driving down the Royal Mile, I asked Rikki where the Police Pass was. He didn't answer at first, so I asked again where it was, and he replied, 'On the hall sideboard.'

I couldn't believe it, and was sure we would have to go back to Glasgow for it, which would make us horribly late. We drove up to the gates, and the head of security came straight over. When he saw Rikki, he saluted and said, 'Nice to see you, Mr Fulton, if you would just park over there.' We both breathed a sigh of relief, and in moments we passed the sentries and were in Holyrood.

There we were met by a housekeeper who first of all showed us to my bedroom. It was vast, with windows from the floor to the ceiling, with a small turret in one corner, inside which I thought there was a writing desk. It was mahogany with a centre which lifted up. It turned out to be a lavatory! I was so lucky because it seemed to be the only one en suite, and all the others were at the far end of a long corridor.

Having admired my room with its enormous double bed, we then went to look at Rikki's bedroom. It was on the other side of the corridor and further down. It looked like a monk's cell! It had a single bed, a chair and a hanging space for clothes. I couldn't see Rikki having a good night there, and went back to my sumptuous bedroom where I found my clothes had been perfectly put away, and as she left to do Rikki's unpacking the housekeeper asked, 'Will it be morning tea for one or two, Madam?'

Madam said very firmly it would be for two.

By now it was time to get ready for the first occasion of our visit. I was glad to get out of the clothes I wore when we were travelling and looked forward to sitting and watching the 'Beating of the Retreat'. I must confess it did seem rather inhospitable as we had only just arrived!

It was not at all what we had expected, having assumed it would all be a military show, but there were singers of Scottish songs and excellent Highland dancing, and even the weather was good. We were almost sorry when we had to return inside.

Once back inside the palace it was time to change for a cocktail party. All the clergy with their wives were to be made welcome at Holyrood. We enjoyed meeting some of them, but very soon a lady-in-waiting suggested we should leave in order to have time to dress for dinner.

There was a formality about dinner and first of all we were presented to the Lord High Commissioner and his Lady. There could be no familiarity between us. They were no longer Norman and Greta, they were 'your Graces' to whom Rikki bowed and I curtsied. We were then taken over, Rikki by a lady-in-waiting and me by an Aide de Comps. He was a naval ADC, charming, courteous and incredibly handsome. He escorted me into the dining room in his dress uniform, complete with a magnificent sword. It really was like being in another world! When dinner was over the ladies withdrew and left the gentlemen to their port and brandy. We then all met up in a rather formal reception in another public room. No one could leave the room until their Graces had retired, which they did before midnight.

What a superb Lord and Lady the MacFarlanes were. They had so much dignity, but also warmth towards whomever they were talking. Lord MacFarlane looked like a handsome aristocrat and Lady MacFarlane was born to be just that, 'her Ladyship'! Perhaps it was having been a Girl Guide Captain that gave her such assurance! She is quite beautiful, slim, with the most lovely face and immaculate hair.

When their Graces left, the guests began to drift towards the door, only it wasn't for an early night – it was to go to the Equerries room, where the party began! Everyone enjoyed it so much that it must have been about 4am before it ended. And then the fun really started.

It was like something out of a French farce. Back in the sleeping quarters, the men prowled the corridor for their wives – or anybody's wife – while all the women were trying to find the lavatories.

In the morning having had a much-needed sleep in that oversize bed, we had our morning tea and went down to breakfast. It was spectacular, with everything you could possibly want set out on a hot tray in silver dishes. Alastair later confided it was his favourite meal of the day, and no wonder.

After such a great start we now had to go to the General Assembly on the Mound.

Their Graces were in the royal car and we were behind them. I was delighted to be met by the ADC, again in dress uniform and sword. Rikki wasn't so sure; he had some reservations about my escort.

We drove up the Royal Mile to the Assembly, which despite the sun, looked very grey, as did the clergymen on the steps. The car drew up and the ADC leapt from his front seat, opened Rikki's door, smacked his gauntlets on the bonnet of the car and said, 'OK Stirling, oot the car.'

We arrived in fits of laughter, which was quite out of place, and Rikki decided the ADC was a terrific fellow!

17

A DIFFERENT THEATRE

After pantomime was over Rikki thought he should see our doctor. He had been in some discomfort for a while, without telling anyone, and was told there was no problem, but he did need a bit of surgery. It turned out the surgeon was someone we met socially and we had spent many pleasant evenings with him and his wife.

I drove Rikki to the Nuffield Hospital, even though we could just as easily have walked there, so close was it to our house – but he needed to be cosseted and to know how much he was loved. The staff there were as marvellous as ever, giving patients reassurance and confidence. When I left Rikki I was told he would be back in his room at 3pm and that I could be there to welcome him when he came round from the anaesthetic. Needless to say I was there on time, but Rikki wasn't.

It was 4pm when a nurse came into the room and apologised; she said Rikki was now in the recovery room and should be back in his room shortly. After two hours a nursing Sister appeared, who said there was nothing to worry about, but Rikki was suffering from low blood pressure, and they would keep him in the recovery room until it improved. She suggested that I go home, and they would phone me when he was back in his room.

I couldn't go. When he came back I wanted to be with him. At 8pm the surgeon came in. He looked pale and very tired and he told me there was no point in my staying. Rikki was now in the intensive-care room, he wasn't conscious and wouldn't know if I was there or not. It would be better if I went home, and he promised he would phone me and tell me when I could see him. I obeyed him, and walked home, not crying, but with an aching empty feeling inside. I couldn't believe what was happening. Rikki had gone in for an everyday operation, in good health, and now they were fighting for his life.

The thought that I might lose him froze my blood, and I walked not in a dream, but a nightmare. Arriving home I just sat numbly waiting to see what would happen next. It was a phone call from the surgeon. Rikki's condition had improved and I could go and see him. This time I took my car. I didn't want another of those walks home and it was now after midnight. Going into the intensive-care room, I found my darling one apparently asleep, but he was moaning, and sometimes cried out with pain. He was being carefully looked after by a very pretty, and obviously skilled nurse, who had been brought in specially to look after him in intensive care. She assured me that he was going to be all right and that the danger of the low blood pressure was now under control and in a short while he would be home.

It was absurd, but the relief of that, mingled with sympathy for the discomfort he was in, made me cry all the tears I had been holding back. I went out of the room, and as I turned into the corridor, there was the surgeon. He must have been worried too, staying from 3pm until 2am but when he saw my tears he said angrily, 'What on earth are you crying for?' I could only say that I hadn't expected Rikki to be in such pain. Then I went home longing for the moment I would welcome him back.

The relief I felt was indescribable. I wasn't going to lose the love of my life after all. At that time I had no religious belief but that day I had prayed, and I made a promise that if Rikki was saved I would return to the Church. On a lighter note I should tell you that the lovely and clever nurse who looked after him in intensive care is now a neighbour of ours. Shortly after she moved here we met her at a friend's party and at one point during the evening Rikki said to her, 'I don't think we've met.' Was he in for a surprise!

It was some days before he was well enough to come home, and he was still very ill and could scarcely walk.

He was very disturbed because he had to start pantomime rehearsals in a few weeks and he was in no fit state to work. Rikki had already decided that it would be his last pantomime – it was such hard work and was taking its toll on his health. My parents had always believed that sea air was recuperating, and thinking it couldn't do any harm, we went to the Pickwick Hotel in Ayr for a week. At first Rikki could only, with some difficulty, walk as far as the front gate, but he was determined, and went a little further each day. He was beginning to look a lot better and had some colour back in his face, and then came the big day when we ventured onto the beach and he got the full benefit of the sea breeze. From then on it became a full recovery.

I hadn't forgotten my promise to the Almighty, and found out the nearest church to our hotel was St Columba's. When I told Rikki I was going there on Sunday he said he would like to go too. We had no idea what it would be like but seeing from the Church noticeboard that the minister's name was Bill Christman, we took that to be a good omen! It was too. He turned out to be young, American, full of enthusiasm and optimism, just what we needed. We were to go home the following Friday, but we enjoyed his sermon and preaching so much we stayed on to the Monday in order to hear him again on the Sunday. He had spoken to us at some length when we first met but this time we invited him and his wife to lunch at the hotel, and had an extremely nice time with them. Bill had certainly aroused our interest, but we knew it wasn't practical to travel to Ayr every Sunday, with the result we did what you're not supposed to, namely, we looked for a minister we could like and admire.

Several devout Christians told us it was the worship in the Church that was important not the preacher, who was immaterial – a point of view we could not accept. For some weeks we visited nearby churches but never felt the inspiration we got from Bill Christman. (Mind you, I think Rikki got a lot of material for I.M. Jolly.)

Funnily enough it was in the BBC canteen that Rikki found the answer. He was complaining about not being able to find a church when the wonderful radio DJ Jimmy Mack said, 'Why don't you come to New Kilpatrick in Bearsden? The minister there is Alastair Symington, and I'm sure you would find him inspiring.' He kindly added, 'I'm an elder there, I could take you next Sunday.'

He did, and how right he had been with his recommendation. The church of New Kilpatrick is lovely, with the most beautiful stained-glass windows, a dream setting for a wedding. More important is the congregation, and kinder more welcoming people you couldn't meet. As for the minister, the Reverend Alastair Symington is magnificent. His sermons are always enthralling and thought-provoking, and as if that isn't enough, he has a sense of humour second to none. We were so grateful to Jimmy Mack, and his beautiful wife Barbara, who sings in the choir every week, for introducing us to many happy years in their church.

We did see Bill Christman again as he invited us to an induction ceremony for himself and a Roman Catholic priest when they became Chaplains to Shotts Prison. We thanked him and accepted, thinking this would be something different. It was! Of course all the prisoners were invited to the service, and rumours of some comic relief began to circulate, with the result that the hall was packed. Someone had overheard that the Reverend Jolly was to take the service and assumed it would be Rikki as I.M. Jolly!

The service was in fact conducted by the Reverend John Jolly, a minister we had already met. He was brought to our house by the press, who then took photographs of himself and Rikki walking along the road deep in conversation with their hands behind their backs, walking away from the cameras. How very good of him to join in the fun.

When we were shown to our seats the Reverend Jolly and the two incumbents were already seated on the platform, and there was a distinct murmuring of discontent and disappointment from the prison congregation, as though they had been conned into attending, and when Rikki appeared there was silence followed by total bewilderment. It was a lovely service, and after it was over Rikki shook countless hands and even signed some autographs. Then the Governor asked if we would like to be shown round the security wing. Of course we said 'yes' but what was a little unexpected was that we were put in the care of a guide who was serving Life Plus. He had been sentenced for killing someone, and the Plus was because he had then killed another prisoner. But you couldn't have found a more charming or informative guide, although I was apprehensive about the number of doors that had been firmly locked behind us. There was no escape!

First of all he showed us his cell, actually a pleasant room, with his books and television. It opened onto a communal lounge where prisoners could meet their visitors. I know there is a school of thought that condemns any comfort in prison, but if you are to have no freedom for the rest of your life, haven't you already lost everything?

We were then given a guided tour of the workshop, where there was only one young man painting a very ugly plaster parrot a vivid emerald green, presumably to add to the shelves of the dozens he had already done. The workshop was well equipped, the walls covered with large knives, Stanley knives, hammers and axes. Rikki loved that kind of thing, and had a similar room at home so he was happy to examine them all. I felt rather safer chatting to the painter.

He was a nervous rather jumpy man but we spoke for a time, at the end of which he brought down one of his emerald parrots and offered it to me. I was so taken aback that I said something like, 'I couldn't accept it, I'm sure you mean to sell it which would be much better for you.'

A hiss behind me from our guide was followed by, 'Take it. You don't want to upset him, he can be violent.'

Heeding the advice, I accepted the parrot with gratitude, and then suggested to Rikki that perhaps it was time to leave. Our guide saw us to the door, where we thanked him for his guided tour, and his advice in the workshop, and then heard the welcome sound of the key turning in the lock and opening the door.

Some years later I would be at the 'Women of Scotland' luncheon where one of the speakers, a very senior prison officer, opened her speech by saying, 'I'm quite sure not one of you ladies has ever been in Shotts Prison.' Rather than raise my arm I sat firmly on my hands.

Rikki and I were so thankful that he was fit enough to do his last pantomime. He really wanted it to be a good one. It had already played the year before in Edinburgh, but it was essential that Rikki should be in the Glasgow production. It was *Cinderella*, and Rikki had written it, directed it and starred in it with Walter Carr. The Edinburgh audiences had been most enthusiastic, but where else could he finish his pantomime career but in Glasgow, and thank goodness he was now well enough to do so.

What I found startling was that Tom Malarky who was in charge of the Glasgow production asked if I would play the Fairy Godmother. When Rikki asked me if I would, he got a resounding 'no'. After the Inverness experience I never ever wanted to play that part again, but he never gave up easily. He said he would write the part for me with some comedy, and make sure my costume fitted this time.

The opportunity to be in Rikki's final pantomime with him

was too good to miss. I accepted and enjoyed every moment, except for the first days when I wasn't happy about the way I was playing the part. I asked Rikki for help, and in five minutes he showed me how it could be improved, and needless to say he was right.

One thing we both found intriguing was that there were two English girls in the cast playing principal boy and girl and after a week's rehearsal they said to some of our friends that they had only just learned, but couldn't believe, that Rikki and I were married. They thought we were so professional it was purely a director/actress relationship. They were, of course, right. To us, theatre was the same as our marriage, Rikki always the one in control, and that's the way I loved it, though I must confess that I did give him my opinion now and again at home!

There couldn't have been a better show than *Cinderella* for Rikki to make his pantomime finale. It was tiring as always, but so very rewarding because the audiences were wonderful. We left the theatre on the last night, smiling. We knew we would be back for next year's pantomime, but we would be in the audience watching others do all the hard work and rush around with the costume changes.

I had hoped that Rikki would be able to stay at home for a good rest, but we became increasingly concerned about Jeeves: he wasn't his lively self and we knew that he, like Jonathon, had a heart murmur. He wasn't in pain but he became tired quickly and sometimes seemed rather breathless. We weren't sure what was the best thing to do for him, but I thought that it had worked for Rikki so perhaps it could work for Jeeves. We took him to Largs for the sea air. Our hotel was in Charles Street, just yards from the sea, and the owners were very kind and understanding about our invalid Westie. He was thoroughly enjoying himself, and we walked along the front many times each day. We didn't go right down to the sea in case he slipped on the pebbly beach, and although we were strolling above it we still got the benefit of the ozone. I don't know if it improved Jeeves' health, but he certainly loved it, and I could see it was doing Rikki a world of good.

We stayed for about ten days before coming home, but after a short time we could see our beloved little dog fading away. One afternoon he went into the garden and lay down on the grass with what sounded like a sigh of relief. He seemed to be asleep, or was he dying? We asked our vet to come to the garden in case Jeeves should wake up in any pain, but he never did wake up. Needless to say we were heartbroken; the house seemed so empty and silent, and how we longed for the sound of barking. After a few days of misery we felt we had to get away, and within hours we were on our way to Pollensa. It was all so easy, we didn't even have to pack – so many summer clothes had been left in the wardrobes of our apartment.

It was truly lovely to be back there, we so needed peace and quiet, and somewhere with no painful memories of our dogs, as there were throughout our home in Glasgow. Rather more visitors came to us than we wanted, but it was probably good for us to have a different circle of friends who took our minds off dogs.

We were now completely free agents and decided to make the most of it. We booked a flight home in six weeks time and we determined to enjoy our prolonged holiday. Our favourite restaurants were as good as ever and the weather was sunshine all the way. At least it was for me, and Rikki enjoyed the shade.

What we hadn't realised was that our third week there coincided with the Glasgow Fair. At the beginning of that year Rikki had recorded what became one of his most popular sketches – the minister who drinks neat gin thinking it's water, becomes absolutely legless and says over and over again, 'It's lovely watter you've got here, where in God's name do you get your watter?'

Can you imagine what it was like when our Glasgow friends arrived? Rikki and I had breakfast of freshly baked croissants with peach jam and coffee on our little balcony, but apart from that we had all our meals out. There wasn't a meal when Rikki didn't have to sign autographs or have his photograph taken with holidaymakers. They were extremely friendly and nice, but even just walking in the street there would be shouts of 'Lovely watter, Rikki, where do you get your watter?'

It was all good fun and normally Rikki would have enjoyed it, but it came at the wrong time. Rikki had been through a near-death experience, he had only just managed to find the strength to do an exhausting pantomime, and that was followed by the death of his beloved dog. He was in no state to be sociable. He decided that until we went home he would stay in the apartment and read his books. That seemed to be a very sensible decision and it seemed to work. For a few days . . .

At that point it had been decided to dig up the road outside our apartment. The local council, very wisely, was going to widen this back road to take the traffic away from the front, which is now a pedestrian precinct with outdoor cafés, restaurants and palm trees – you might think you were in Cannes, it's most attractive – but did they *have* to start when Rikki needed a rest? The noise was unbelievable, and as Majorca is a volcanic island, digging up a road is not easy. They used pile drivers, metal barrows they could throw the rocks into and those awful drills – in fact anything that would make a din. They started at 8am and finished at 8pm every day, Sundays included. Rikki was now a nervous wreck and I was seriously worried about him. I arranged the first available flight and took him home.

Gradually the peace and quiet of the house and garden worked their magic and he began to relax. There was no intrusive noise whatsoever as our road had by now been closed off at the far end, putting a stop to the rat run avoiding the traffic lights on the main road. Now we had an oasis of calm, and sometimes it was difficult to realise we were only fifteen minutes from the city centre. When Rikki felt fully recovered there was one project on his mind, to sell our holiday apartment. This he did in just a few days, and then we wondered, what do we do now? We still enjoyed Pollensa and didn't want to stop going there but staying out of the busy town centre was now necessary. The next time we went there we stayed in a hotel at the far end of the bay, and what a good choice it was. The Hotel Illa D'or was all we could ask for. We even gave the receptionists the names of people we didn't want to see, and if they phoned, or came looking for us, they were politely told that we were not staying in the hotel.

Whenever I think of our favourite hotels there is one that immediately springs to mind – the Banchory Lodge Hotel. Banchory is a charming place, and the hotel is owned by Maggie and Duguld Jaffray, an extraordinary couple. There is never a dull moment when they are around and their stories of the show-business personalities who have stayed there would make your hair stand on end. One unwelcome guest insisted on an invitation to one of their big parties, then asked to be in the cabaret, enjoyed their hospitality over a weekend, then sent them a bill for his 'Professional Services'.

We got to know them when Rikki was doing the second run at the Edinburgh Festival of *A Wee Touch O' Class*, which then went on tour. Our friend Anne Kidd had played the Marchioness opposite Rikki who, despite being a married man, was besotted by her. When the play went on for the second year Anne wasn't free to do it again, so guess who played it second time around?

I loved every minute of it. In fact, if I was asked, 'What was the happiest moment of my life?', it would have been in that play – only it wasn't just a moment, it happened every night for many weeks.

There was a scene where Rikki and I were alone onstage, talking at cross-purposes. I thought I was talking about a bovine animal, and he thought I was talking about his wife, so that when I asked him 'When did the old cow die?' his reaction to that brought screams of laughter which lasted for some time. That was my happiest moment. We were sitting on a sofa looking into each other's eyes while we waited for the laughter he had created to quieten so we could continue the dialogue. I could turn upstage to let him see the love in my eyes, his sparkled in reply, but he still had to keep the audience laughing!

When the tour went to Aberdeen Rikki refused to stay in the town, which is why we were in Banchory – and what a happy choice it was. As a matter of fact Rikki had to alter his opinion of Aberdeen audiences. They were just marvellous, and we were there for two weeks, completely sold out. There seemed to be two different groups, one audience which enjoyed plays and the classics, and the other which preferred Variety.

While we were there we knew that the young Prince Edward was playing a leading part in Pinero's *The Magistrate* at Haddo House, near Aberdeen. It's a very aristocratic home and presents plays and musical concerts in its theatre. It seemed that for once the tickets were not going like the usual hot cakes and we were told that Prince Edward was overheard explaining, 'There's a chap called Rikki Fulton in Aberdeen and he seems to be getting our audiences.'

I was relieved the tour was going well because it had had a bad start. The venue the Edinburgh Festival had chosen for Rikki's return was the Leith Town Hall, and it would seat hundreds more than the previous year at the Churchill Theatre.

Rikki always drove Clem to wherever the play was being presented and the ever-punctual Clem was always waiting on the pavement when the car arrived. The previous week we had been in Perth, so of course Rikki drove the three of us back to Glasgow.

Clem lived for many years in Hyndland Road, in a top flat opposite the tennis courts where he always had a pair of binoculars handy by the window in case on the days the girls were playing there was a strong wind blowing their skirts about.

To call Clem a ladies' man would be something of an understatement.

That Monday afternoon there was no sign of him outside his bed sitter in Cleveden Road. We began to worry a bit – it was so unlike him to be late. Rikki left the car and went round the back of the house, where he found the curtains closed, and no amount of ringing the bell and knocking on the door brought any response. Fortunately at that moment a lady drove into the small car park and she turned out to be in charge of the bed sitters which were rented, and most importantly she had their keys.

She gave Rikki the one to Clem's and he let himself in. The room was in darkness but he managed to cross it and opened the curtain, and then he found Clem. He was lying on the floor beside a water heater which he had pulled from the wall when he fell, and it looked as though he had been dead for some hours. Rikki must have been in a state of shock but he came outside and calmly told the caretaker not to go into the room, but to phone the police at once. He told her what had happened and apologised for not staying with her, explaining that it was our first night in the Edinburgh Festival and we had to get there as quickly as possible.

We didn't speak for some time, each with our own thoughts of Clem. A sad man in many ways, and a loner, I hoped he didn't know what was happening just before he died. He could be very disciplined when he was working, and wouldn't touch alcohol during the week if he was in a play, but come Saturday night and all day Sunday, he more than made up for his week's abstinence! He also suffered from hypertension, and as he had been hospitalised for it quite recently, perhaps a sudden death was inevitable.

We were on the motorway before we started talking and that of course was about how we were going to get the play on with one of the characters missing. Somehow Rikki had to solve that before we arrived at the theatre because there was no understudy.

Clem had played one of the tutors which Mr Jenner – Rikki – employed in an effort to make himself a 'Gentleman'. Clem had been the Master of Elocution. Rikki cut the scene out and managed to get laughs by dropping some of the Master's lines into his own dialogue, and everyone else mentally blocked out the cues they used to get from Clem and went straight ahead with the script that remained. The audience was blissfully unaware that anything was wrong, but I can assure you that none of us will ever forget *that* first night.

Rikki might no longer have been in pantomime but he was still doing *Scotch and Wry* and apart from that he was still in the news. One morning in 1991 he had a letter from the Prime Minister, it was John Major at the time, saying that he was thinking to recommend to Her Majesty that Rikki become an Officer of the Order of the British Empire, and if he did, would Rikki accept? This was followed by two small boxes which had to be ticked, one for Yes and one for No. We were surprised and rather excited by this, and Rikki filled in his reply and sent it off. Absolutely nothing happened. We watched our mail carefully but nothing else arrived. We reconciled ourselves to the fact that by mistake Rikki must have ticked the No box instead of the Yes one.

It was many weeks later when we had a phone call from the press asking if they could come to the house and photograph Rikki. He asked them for what reason, and was told that the Birthday Honours List would be published the following day and they had seen he was being given an OBE. Apparently our no news was good news after all.

18

MEET THE ARTIST

Some months later we were summoned to Buckingham Palace but needless to say this it did not go exactly to plan. We thought we would spend a few days in London, and spend it in style, so we booked into the Ritz Hotel. We did go to the theatre, but only to matinées because we enjoyed dinner at the Ritz. I did eat rather more than Rikki; he stayed with his plain three-course meal, while I liked all the tit-bits they served between courses. The night before we went to the Palace these were particularly good, including oysters, something Rikki wouldn't contemplate. And yes, I wakened in the morning feeling very ill.

Thankfully Rikki didn't have time to notice because he was wearing the kilt for the Investiture and it always took both of us some time to get him sorted with all the bits and pieces that are needed even for a day kilt outfit. In the car that was taking us to the Palace I stared fixedly out of the window, away from Rikki. It was a short drive and the moment we were within the gates Rikki was whisked away, and for once I was glad about it, and thankful that he hadn't seen the colour of my face.

On my own now, I went up the stairs to the ballroom where the ceremony would be held. I was in a fragile state and not prepared to find that the costumed men lining either side of the stairway, which I had thought were statues, turned out to be living breathing guardsmen!

Being one of the first to arrive I was shown to the front row and was very pleased when a lady, on her own, sat beside me. We started talking, and she told me that she and her husband lived and worked abroad now and they were so delighted to come home for his award in the Honours List. After we had talked I was aware that she was looking at me very closely and she said, 'Are you feeling all right?'

As I was now apparently an interesting shade of green she told me that she was a nurse and if I felt really ill she would take me out of the room. The fact that she was so friendly and capable helped me relax for the first time that day.

Rikki was given his beribboned medal quite early in the ceremony, and I hoped that Her Majesty wouldn't recognise him as the man who had given her 'The Nod' in Holyrood. And if I were to throw up on the carpet it would only compound things and we'd be scored off the royal sherry list! As soon as we could escape we took a taxi back to the Ritz where Rikki asked them to send for a doctor. He arrived quickly and gave me one of those magic injections which seem to have an immediate effect. The hotel was noncommittal about the oysters though they did take the cost of that meal off our bill. I haven't been back to the Ritz again – I much prefer the Savoy, and I never order oysters.

Rikki had some more surprises to come. First of all when we returned home there was a letter waiting for him from Strathclyde University asking if he would accept an honorary Doctorate of Letters. It didn't take any persuasion and that was followed by an honorary Doctorate of Arts from the University of Abertay, Dundee. Then the University of St Andrews gave him a second honorary Doctorate of Letters. He was thrilled to bits with all three though it took him some time to become used to being addressed as Doctor Fulton.

I was glad when we set off for Puerto de Pollensa because it had been a very busy year and I thought Rikki had become rather tired and sometimes irritable. He astonished me one night as we were going down the staircase on our way to dinner. Rikki, who was in front of me suddenly swung round and shouted at me with anger, 'Don't look at me like that.' I smiled and pointed out that as I was walking behind him he couldn't possibly see the expression on my face. Then I saw the expression on his. He wasn't joking, he meant it. Our evening meal was more subdued than usual, but when we went for our late-night stroll it was as though the argument had never happened and it wasn't mentioned again. I was glad to learn from Rikki that he had booked our next visit to Pollensa before we flew home, so that must surely mean that he had enjoyed our holiday after all.

One other short holiday which I know he loved was the one we spent with Dugald and Maggie in their Banchory Lodge Hotel, to celebrate our Silver Wedding in 1994, and it couldn't have been better. The two of them were the epitome of kindness and generosity, and we had a truly wonderful time. It was one anniversary that even Rikki couldn't forget!

We returned to Pollensa, which never changes, but from the word go it was different and I realised it wasn't the place or the lovely hotel, it was us! For the first time Rikki didn't come into the port, he preferred to sit on the hotel terrace for the entire day; he would chat to friends, and he slept quite a lot. There was no doubt he was depressed, and very worried about it. He couldn't think what was wrong.

By sheer chance we were introduced to a doctor and his wife who had just arrived. We talked for some time during which he told us that he specialised in dealing with manic depression. Rikki's eyes lit up and he asked if they could have a talk sometime. I was afraid that he was about to be shot down in flames, but on the contrary, the doctor said he would be delighted, and that the four of us should meet for a drink after dinner. This we did. After-dinner drinks were a highlight of the day – friends would take a table, others would join them, then they would drift away to other tables, so by the end of the night you would probably have talked to everyone there.

The four of us settled down to a very serious discussion when we were interrupted by a couple from Glasgow that we had been meeting for years in Pollensa. Seeing the four of us together they decided to join us. That of course put paid to the talk we had been looking forward to having. We offered them drinks, which we hoped they would refuse, but they didn't. We had to resort to polite conversation which became very boring. At last they left, and told mutual friends that it was the first time they hadn't felt welcome at our table, but if you gatecrash a medical consultation what else can you expect?

Rikki explained that he thought he was suffering from depression and it was making him angry. There was no possible reason for it. He had absolutely nothing to be depressed about. The doctor was understanding and made many helpful comments but above all he hoped Rikki would seek medical advice when we went home.

This I knew he would do as he was always an obedient patient, did as he was told, and always took his medication. I was so grateful to the doctor we had just met, for reassuring Rikki. I hoped it would help him to relax and begin to enjoy his holiday. And Rikki did seem better with each day that passed. Now we were enjoying the company of our special friends, Tom and Jeanette, and Bert and Jean. They had known each other for many years and always came on this holiday as a foursome. Their company really made our holiday, and now that Rikki was feeling sociable again it felt as though things were back to normal. He even started to come into the port again and it was a joy to have his company. We had a very pleasant morning there and enjoyed the walk back to the hotel for lunch.

While we were having lunch a lady came over and asked Rikki, politely, if she could have his autograph. He smiled and said, 'With pleasure.'

He took a pen from his pocket, but it wasn't the one he liked to use for signing, which I had seen in the bedroom, so I told him I would get it for him. Our room was on the first floor, and running upstairs, picking up the pen and running downstairs took no time at all. Back at the table the lady was no longer there.

When he saw me he got to his feet and shouted in temper at me. He told me that I was being ridiculous – what difference did it make which pen he used? He had signed the autograph with the one he had, while I was running around the hotel like an idiot, he told me. The shouting went on for a considerable time, but I now knew enough not to say a word. I sat there quietly and when at last he did sit down, he shared my silence.

For the first time I was glad when our holiday was over, and not surprised that on the morning we left Rikki said he no longer liked Pollensa and would never return. I could only hope that he would feel much better when he was home. It took a little time but gradually after a few days of peace, the Rikki I knew and loved with all my heart came home.

Thankfully the actor and comedian also returned and Rikki and Jack were busier than ever. Looking at a typical work schedule I wonder how they survived! On our return from Pollensa Rikki was straight into rehearsals for *Scotch and Wry*.

In the summer he and Jack were starring in *King's High* at the King's Theatre. If you add all the scriptwriting that's involved in those performances to the actual work on stage it's a punishing schedule, and made me wonder if Rikki's depression and bouts of temper when we were on holiday had been the result of simply working too hard.

It was unbelievably good to have him back to his usual self and life returned to a semblance of normality, which is as much as we could ask for.

Our dogs had always been the joy of our lives. We were so heartbroken when first Jonathon and then Jeeves died that after some time we realised we had to get two more. The silence of the house was becoming too loud! We were told of a lady in

Kilmarnock, a judge at dog shows, who bred Westies and knew everything there was to know about them. I phoned her, to be told that there would be a litter in about two weeks, and if we would like we could see them, choose the two we wanted and we could collect them in six to eight weeks' time.

In due course we met them and what a litter they were! We did the same as before and chose a beautiful confident puppy, and then the smallest one who didn't seem sure what being in the world was all about. As well as being so happy to meet the pups, we were equally happy to meet their owner, Anne, and her husband, Chic. We could have listened all day to their dog talk, and looked forward to seeing them again.

We loved having these two pups and how sad we were when Jamie, who was the smaller of the two, died unexpectedly of a heart attack in the garden. We were just so glad that we still had the adorable Jake, and that he seemed so fit. Our late-night walks would go on for some time we thought, and they did.

A few years later Rikki and Jack were once more working at the King's. Jake and I would always go to the front door with Rikki to wave them off. Next on the agenda would be Jake's meal for which he was always enthusiastic. Particularly that night, he ran all around the room as I prepared it giving squeals of delight when he smelled what he was going to get. I was just about to take it from the table and put it on the floor for him when he made the most enormous leap up to the table and at a great height gave a yelp. I caught him as he fell, he made a slight murmur in my arms and was dead.

I could hardly believe it. He had been so full of life only seconds ago. I laid him gently on the floor and felt for his heartbeat. There wasn't one, but I thought there was a tiny pulse beat. I was sure he was dead, but what if that tiny beat meant he could be revived? Who could I ask? There were no vets nearby – practically all our neighbours were doctors. I phoned Connie and Bob who came straight away and they were with me in minutes. I can't thank them enough for their understanding – they too are animal lovers and have the most exquisite Siamese cats. They confirmed that Jake was dead, and when I told them about the tiny beat I thought I had heard I asked them if it could have been my own, as the pulse on my wrist was over his heart. They said that was quite likely. I thanked them for putting my mind at rest and asked if they would come through to the drawing room for a drink. Bob said it was a good idea and that Connie and I should go through and he would join us shortly. It was a little while before he came in because what he had been doing was shutting Jake's eyes and jaws.

The three of us were now all thinking of how Rikki was going to feel when I told him what had happened. Bob had done wonders with Jake, who now looked as though he was very happily asleep. When they left I could only think how incredibly lucky we were to have them not only as friends but neighbours.

I wrapped Jake's travelling rug round him but left him where I had laid him after his fall, and waited for Rikki.

When I saw the taxi I went to the door and opened it the moment he arrived. We had our usual hugging session, and I handed him the brandy and Canada Dry he loved at the end of a day's work. I had it ready on the sideboard for him and while we were still in the hall I asked what his night had been like. He was exuberant, and he said the audience had been the best ever and he had loved every moment of playing to them. He then went on to describe his favourite reactions from them. When he finished I said gently that I was so glad he had that kind of night because I had the saddest of news for him.

'Jake died tonight.'

He was stunned. All he could say was, 'How?'

I told him what had happened and added that Jake had died of joy and excitement, not a bad way for a loved happy dog to go. Rikki asked where he was, I took his hand and we went into the kitchen together.

Bob truly had worked wonders. Jake looked unbelievably beautiful, happy and contented. Rikki caught his breath when he saw him and gently stroked his lovely white head. I suggested that Rikki should put him in his kennel, which he did with infinite gentleness. Now what? There would be no late-night walk that night or any other, and as neither of us could face a meal, we just went upstairs, got into bed, held hands and cried ourselves to sleep. Just before that Rikki asked what was to happen to Jake, and I told him that when Connie confirmed he was dead I phoned the vet who offered to come and collect him, but there was no way he could go without Rikki saying goodbye to him. She understood and said she would be round first thing in the morning.

'I'm not getting up till lunchtime,' Rikki very wisely said.

Mrs Cowie arrived around nine. She was very kind and after a few words Jake, still in his rug, was carried out to her car, out of our home forever, but never, never, out of our hearts. It was a sad day, but at the end of it Rikki went on stage and made people laugh.

It reminded me of the time we went to see Jimmy Logan in pantomime. He was such a good Dame and the audience loved him. What the audience didn't know was that he had just been told terrifyingly tragic news about his personal life by his then wife. Without any warning she had left him and returned to Inverness, taking the twins Jimmy adored with her. Her parting shot was that he wasn't their father.

Rikki and I were overjoyed when Jimmy later married Angela, who loved him and cared for him in a way I don't believe he had ever known before.

Rikki was missing Jake every waking moment and I knew something had to be done. I phoned Anne to ask if she had any pups for sale and was startled to hear that she didn't breed West Highland terriers any more, she now bred Shetland Collies. She didn't know of any Westie litters that were due, but we had just missed a great one. When she started breeding Shetlands she gave her Westies to a friend, another judge of dogs, who had a farm at Kilwinning – and that was the litter we had missed.

The pups' paws scarcely touched the ground before they were sold, all except one which they were keeping as a show dog and at stud. Could she be persuaded to sell him, I asked? Anne didn't think so, but said she would phone her and tell her how happy Jake and Jamie had been, as a reference. I didn't tell Rikki, I just fervently hoped Anne would be successful. She was! She phoned me that night to say her friend, Betty, had agreed to sell him. I'm sure it was for Rikki's sake that they came to our rescue, guessing what it would mean to him. The pup was fifteen weeks old and was called Hamish – we could collect him the next day.

Rikki came home, trying not to show how miserable he was; thankfully we were again able to have our late-night meal. We talked as usual about the show, who we had met that day, and who had phoned, and then I asked him if we could go to Kilwinning the next day.

'What on earth for?'

'That's where we have to go to collect our new West Highland pup,' I told him.

His face was a study, every known emotion seemed to cross it. After some time he said, 'Are you quite mad?' but he was smiling.

Rikki had recently bought a new Jaguar so a run to Kilwinning suited him very well. Betty had given us clear directions as to how to find the farm, and for once we didn't get lost. We drove into a neat and spacious farmyard and the barking started from every side. Betty was there and we admired all the dogs – they were so attractive and friendly, but they were all adults. Betty said she would get Hamish, who was shut in on the opposite side of the yard. We stayed where we were and the moment she opened the door, a white ball of fluff shot like a rocket towards us; it jumped and barked and licked. Hamish was over the moon and we joined him. I hadn't seen Rikki enjoy himself like that for a long time and I prayed this tiny creature was going to keep him happy. I was so grateful to Betty for letting us have him.

We gave her a cheque and then started to learn about Hamish's diet and the frequency of his meals. I suppose we were talking for some time and when we stopped there was no sign of Hamish. Betty called him and at that point Rikki said, 'That dog isn't a Hamish.' I asked, 'Who is he then?'

Rikki's voice was determined. 'He is Jake, mark two.'

Whatever his name was he still could not be found. We searched the yard and checked that he hadn't gone back to bed. Now we were really worried – surely he hadn't run away, he had seemed so happy – then we heard a polite puppy bark and there he was, sitting very comfortably in the passenger seat of the Jaguar. Knowing him now as we do I'm only surprised he didn't want to drive. That was the moment Jake mark two took over our lives and ruled us with a rod of iron.

It was rather difficult house-training him as he was used to the freedom of the farm, but after six months he finally got the hang of it.

Rikki's next part was something quite different for him. He went into an episode of *Rab C. Nesbitt*, playing a ghastly old man who made Rab C. look as though he was dressed by Burberry! He was looking forward to working with his chum, Gregor Fisher. With his dog to welcome him home, and spending the working days with friends, things were looking good. It was heart-warming to see him go out in the morning with such enthusiasm.

Everything seemed splendid, until the last day of filming. He came home as though the world had crashed about him, and when I asked him what had happened he said in a very flat, sad voice, 'I can't remember lines any more.'

One of the scenes he was in had to be shot 23 times. That was unheard of for Rikki, who always prided himself on being called

'One-take Fulton', and he would have been mortified if there had to be a second shot. My heart broke for him – what was happening to him?

It took many days before he recovered from that, but he did, and came up with an excellent idea. He would start painting again. Before we met up he painted a tremendous amount, it was almost like a compulsive hobby. He gave all his work away, and friends began to say to him that they had redecorated and would he do a painting to match the new colour scheme? And he would – he loved it. I had never known him to paint and it seemed that this could be the answer to his future retirement.

The next day we went into one of the best art shops and were lucky enough to be looked after by the owner who gave us the right advice and got us kitted up with everything Rikki might need. We arrived home with it all, including the easel, and wondered quite where we could put it. When Rikki had painted before he used a room upstairs which is now my dressing room, and I was perfectly happy to move and let him use it again, but he had never liked the light there. We settled on a room downstairs at the back of the house where he would have absolute peace, and it looked onto the back garden and got all the sun in the morning. In no time he was settled there very happily. I was still very concerned about him, though. He was becoming forgetful, but perhaps that was the result of having spent his life remembering everything!

19

JOYOUS REUNION WITH OUR TEACHERS

One thing I was glad about was that Rikki was doing a lot of walking. He took Jake for two good walks every day. They both loved it, and Rikki enjoyed talking to the neighbours and anyone else who was out with a dog. He always had a story to tell me when he came home.

We each had a most welcome reunion with two ladies we had met either in school or college. Mine was with Miss Ida Watt of the Edinburgh College of Drama. We met by chance when Rikki and I went to a theatre in Edinburgh and she was sitting near us with her husband – she was now Mrs John Anderson. She had scarcely changed at all! She is small and petite with dark hair and the most brilliant, sparkling brown eyes, but it's her personality that I find fascinating. She is interested in everything. She produces plays in Edinburgh and she is so vivacious and inspiring and informative that I can imagine people forming a queue to be in them. She is such an extraordinarily talented lady that I'm not at all surprised that Rikki fell in love with her at our first meeting, which fortunately was the first of many.

And Rikki also finally found the English teacher he had loved, thanks to Una MacLean. She had just moved into a flat in Hyndland Road in Glasgow when we met at a dinner party. She was keeping us all amused, as only Una can, by telling us about her new neighbours, and one in particular called Joyce who had been a teacher and then held a senior position at Jordanhill College for which she was given an OBE. One of the things that impressed Una was Joyce's beautiful speaking voice. Rikki, who had been listening with great interest, asked if her surname was Moffat, and Una said it was. So there we were – the woman for whom he had been looking for so many years lived just around the corner.

Joyce and Una came for dinner the following week and Joyce and Rikki had a joyful reunion. She had such an influence on him when she taught him English that he never forgot it. As well as inspiring him to read even more widely than before, she gave him his first theatrical role playing Shakespeare's Sir Toby Belch.

I told them of the coincidence of my meeting Ida Watt just a week earlier, to which Joyce said, 'Dear Ida, she came and taught at Jordanhill when I was there.'

The next week we took Joyce to Edinburgh to meet Ida and the four of us had lunch together. The conversation never flagged!

Rikki and I also had a coincidence in our own lives. When all my things arrived in our home Rikki liked a photograph I had to have taken for *The Mousetrap* programme. He framed it and put it on the mantelpiece in his study. It sat at the opposite end from a photograph of himself. I was intrigued by the fact that they looked like a matching set. After weeks of wondering I asked Rikki who had taken his photograph, but he couldn't remember. I asked if it had been Mark Gudgeon and he said that's just who it was. When we got our diaries out we discovered we had been there on the same day: Rikki, late morning, me, early afternoon. We had missed each other by two hours! Presumably the Fates decided we had to wait for our time to come.

That was all a long time ago – my present concern was for Rikki's health. If he was walking with Jake, painting, or playing his beloved piano he seemed perfectly happy, but there were times when he would sleep a lot, or even sit staring into space. He used to be an avid reader but now he never opened a book, and no longer read the papers. He loved going to the theatre and meeting up with the Chums, though he sometimes got them muddled up. No one seemed to mind and he so enjoyed the company.

We were so lucky to have the most excellent doctors who were also our good friends. They are brother and sister, and Rikki usually went to Paul. They got on extremely well and had a great regard for each other, and if Paul had a few minutes free he sometimes phoned to say he'd be round at lunchtime. We'd just have a snack and were always so pleased to see him. One day when he arrived, Rikki was upstairs playing the piano, so I was able to tell Paul how worried I was.

When Rikki came down I was glad that he told Paul about his depression, and Paul thought he could find some tablets which would help. From then on he monitored Rikki closely and it was such a relief to have an expert involved. Sometimes I would think Rikki was improving and then he would have a mood swing and fly into a temper. You never knew from one hour to the next how he was going to be, and it must have been absolute hell for Rikki. I'm sure he couldn't begin to fathom what was going on any more than I could. We were both totally lost, but at least we were in it together and the love we shared made anything bearable.

I went to see Paul at his surgery and told him things were getting worse; nothing Rikki was taking seemed to make any difference. Then I knew I had to ask the question that scared the life out of me.

'Paul, is it Alzheimer's?' There was silence. I looked at him, and he nodded. That was the end of my happiness forever.

'What do we do now?' I asked.

Paul explained that we must get him specialist care and put him on tablets specifically for Alzheimer's, and with that he took charge.

I drove home with a surprisingly clear head. Only one thing

mattered, that Rikki's life should be made as comfortable as it could possibly be. I also decided not to tell him, what good would that do? It would only frighten him, and I reckoned he was scared enough. He was watching from the window as I drove in; he'd been doing that quite a lot recently, and it was heaven to be held in his embrace. My thoughts were that however long we had together, we would be happy.

Rikki hadn't lost his appetite, loved mealtimes and they became more like intimate parties which we both enjoyed.

One night at supper I broached the subject of a holiday, which startled him. But before he could start worrying, I said that as neither of us wanted to go abroad, perhaps we could find somewhere we could drive to, and take Jake with us. He was most enthusiastic about the idea, and I told him Ida had mentioned an excellent hotel she went to every year. It was in Pitlochry and was called The Green Park Hotel – and she had seen guests there with their dogs. What a favour she did us. Had we been asked to describe our dream hotel in Scotland it would have sounded just like Green Park, and the icing on the cake was the Pitlochry Festival Theatre, which had different plays on each night and different matinées each day. You might know Joyce also went every year!

We had a glorious time at the hotel, which sits on the edge of Loch Faskally with beautiful views. Inside it is so welcoming that even on your first visit you feel you've come home. It's owned by two generations of the McMenemie family, and do they know how to run it! Before we left we counted them and their staff as friends. It was Jake's first holiday but he told us privately he would certainly be back. It was certainly our answer for future holidays. Rikki loved the superb food and the feeling of both companionship and privacy. It was hard to believe we now knew somewhere to which we could escape, and it certainly did Rikki a lot of good.

We arrived home to learn that Paul had arranged for us to

meet Dr Johnny Woods, and what a blessing that turned out to be, and also Mr David Scott the psychologist who would see Rikki once a week. I was so thankful for these remarkable men. Dr Woods prescribed for Rikki and had tests done, and Rikki went to David Scott every Tuesday afternoon and thoroughly enjoyed it. Suddenly instead of being on my own with Rikki's illness there was now a whole team effort, and what a difference that made.

Gradually, though, in spite of all their efforts, he got worse. His walking was not as good and his memory was failing. He now had difficulty finding the right words which understandably made him very angry. And yet whatever happened, our love was surviving strongly. The sad thing was that Rikki didn't want me out of his sight, and when I had to go out, on my return he would run down the steps in tears and thank me so much for coming back. I tried hard to reassure him but it was no good.

I felt it was time I read up on Alzheimer's so I bought books on the subject. The first thing I learned was that I was seriously wrong. They all said how important it is for patients to be told they have the illness. I would tell him at the first opportunity but where and when?

As usual Rikki solved it for me. We were finishing lunch one Tuesday just before he went to see David, and with his impeccable timing he said, 'Katie, what's wrong with me?'

I said, 'My darling, you have Alzheimer's.'

He looked horrified. 'But that's an old man's illness,' and then he collapsed. There was nothing I could do except hold him close; he was in bits but I knew David would put them together for him. Some hours later he came home and he was calmer. I don't know what David said but it certainly worked. It seemed strange to be able to talk about this vile cruel illness but the fact that we could gave us both a sense of relief. Now we really were in it together.

The next thing that shattered Rikki was the death, in 2001, of his dear friend, Jack Milroy. They seemed to have been friends forever. I used to love it when neither of them was working and Jack would come round for afternoon tea. He loved the tiered cake stands with the requisite sandwiches, scones and cakes. I always set it in the dining room because I don't think men can be bothered with balancing cups and plates on their knees. It certainly wasn't acceptable to Francie and Josie. I loved hearing their laughter coming in waves from the dining room as they reminisced. Neither Mary nor I ever intruded on the Boys' Afternoons. Rikki had tremendous affection for Jack and was deeply saddened when he died. Mary asked Rikki to speak at Jack's funeral and he said he would be honoured to do so. I just hoped he would be able to handle the emotion of the day.

Because Rikki was making a speech we were placed in the front row on the left-hand seats, which meant that Rikki would walk right across the room to the lectern and back. I just hoped his legs wouldn't let him down. Mary had arranged a lovely service and the crematorium was packed with Jack's many friends in show business and the press were out in force. I knew that for the first time in his life Rikki was feeling nervous about talking to an audience, or in this case a congregation, but when the time came he walked to the lectern looking confident. Although his speech about Jack was perhaps more halting than usual, he got through it. It was only at the very end when he was talking about Mary and looking straight at her that he collapsed.

It was the misery of the one left on their own that he could never cope with. Mary was the first on her feet to help him and he was brought back to his seat to recover. Fortunately he quickly forgot about it, but the press didn't. I was phoned and asked if it was true that Rikki was suffering from Parkinson's disease and I truthfully said 'no', but it didn't end there. The reporter ran through other illnesses and when he got to Alzheimer's I didn't know what to say. If I denied it, before long it would obviously be shown to be a lie, and thankfully Rikki no longer read the papers, so I said 'yes'. The article which appeared the next day wasn't at all harmful; in fact, it was rather nice.

Rikki's walking was my main concern. The speech difficulty didn't bother us at all as we always knew what the other was thinking. Rikki refused to give up his walks with Jake and there was no point in insisting. As far as I was concerned whatever he wanted he could have, and that included his daily menu!

One day when I was shopping for groceries I came home to an empty house, but that didn't disturb me. I presumed Rikki had taken Jake out. A short while later the phone rang. It was Mary Milroy to tell me that Rikki had had a bad fall and was in the Western Infirmary. Apparently he had been out with Jake and had tripped on the pavement opposite Anniesland College, hit his head and passed out. Some students saw what had happened and rushed to help him but finding him unconscious wisely phoned for an ambulance. I thanked Mary for telling me and said I would go straight to the Western, but the second big worry was, what had happened to Jake?

Again Mary was a fund of information – the gentleman who lived next to the corner had most kindly taken Jake into his home and that's where I would find him. It seems that when the ambulance arrived people gathered round and someone had told Mary what had happened, knowing that she would contact me. I am so grateful that she did, otherwise I would have gone out of my mind with worry as to where they were. I got back into the car and went to collect Jake. He must have got such a fright when Rikki fell, but now he was jumping about having been so very kindly cared for. It really is amazing how people, often strangers, save the day in a crisis.

I put Jake in the house and drove to Rikki. He was wide awake now and I was glad he remembered nothing about his fall. His face had been cleaned up and was badly bruised but thankfully he hadn't broken any bones. Now even he conceded that the walks with Jake had reached their end. I wondered if the bad bash on his head had exacerbated the Alzheimer's, but there was no way of telling. I was just so glad to get him home again.

He continued to enjoy his weekly visit to David Scott, though he said he worried a bit about what the staff and patients thought when they passed David's door and all that could be heard were gales of laughter! He found David a delight, and said he was the best audience anyone could ask for.

In the early Spring we made a documentary on living with Alzheimer's for Kirsty Wark. The Alzheimer's Society were very glad we did it.

Dr Woods called regularly, often changing Rikki's medication and Paul was helpful, as he always had been. In spite of everything they were doing I could see that Rikki was continuing to get worse. He now got lost in the house, unable to remember which room was which or what its use was. The piano playing was over as was the painting. I wasn't surprised when Dr Woods said he wanted to take Rikki into Gartnavel Royal for assessment, but I had a terrible feeling of foreboding.

On the day of his appointment I told Rikki that Dr Woods wanted to do some tests and that he might have to stay there for a day or two. I honestly thought I was telling the truth but I was so wrong – Rikki would be there for seven weeks.

He wasn't in the main building of Gartnavel Royal, but in one of the houses in the grounds down by Crow Road. Called Timbury House, it was all on ground level and set in attractive gardens. The staff were not only efficient but very caring and it certainly wasn't their fault that Rikki was so unhappy. I knew he would be, he hated being away from home. I had come to the conclusion that his outbursts in Pollensa had been the first signs of Alzheimer's but I think they were brought on by his insecurity at being away from home. I dreaded to think how he would cope with this situation, not only was he away from home but he was on his own.

I stayed with him so that I could unpack his case and see him settled in his room. I hated leaving him but the nursing staff were waiting to see him. We kissed goodbye and I promised I would be back the next day. As I drove home a cloud of fear was gathering around me but even through that I had to accept the irony of it all. From our house there's a clear view of Gartnavel Royal, and often our guests would ask what that impressive-looking building was. They always got the same answer from Rikki. He would explain that it was a hospital which specialised in all forms of dementia and he would finish by saying how handy it was – when he went completely gaga he only had to cross the road! That's why I was so glad he was at the other end of the grounds. If he had been in the main building he would have been looking into his own front windows, and I can guess the effect that would have had on him.

It felt very strange to be alone in the house. Like most people we had an established routine before we went to bed. I would lock the inner doors and Rikki would lock the front and back doors, then we would go upstairs with our arms around each other. Rikki had a strange sort of fixation about keys, which shook me the first time I saw it happen. We had both been fast asleep when Rikki let out a yell, sat up straight in bed and clutched his throat.

'Rikki, what's wrong?' I asked, but he couldn't reply, just pointed to his throat and made a sort of gurgling sound, his face panic-stricken. I knew that somehow I had to calm him down, so I put my arms around him and quietly told him there was nothing to be afraid of, that he'd had a very bad dream but it was all over now, it was finished. I could feel the tension easing and his face beginning to relax and at last he took his hands away from his throat. After a short time I asked him what had happened and in a quiet rather croaky voice he told me they were trying to choke him. I asked who 'they' were, and he said, 'The keys. I swallowed them and they were choking me.'

That recurring nightmare would happen at least once a week

and sometimes more and when he started to develop Alzheimer's the daymares began. He kept losing the keys. He would unlock the front door in the morning, we would have breakfast and Rikki would go upstairs to shower and dress. When he was ready to take Jake for his walk I used to hear him stamping about and shouting, and it was made clear that the keys were not to be found. Rikki would be frantic, and I joined in the search but to no avail – there was no sign of them. Then I tried to remember when they were last seen; the front door was unlocked so they must be around there somewhere. I started to retrace all the moves we had made that morning and went upstairs. There I hit the jackpot and came down with them in my hand. Rikki was delighted and asked where they were found. I told him they had been in his dressing-gown pocket. I was glad that they had been found and hoped that it wouldn't happen again, but it did, every single day. At least I never had to search again, all I had to do was shout, 'Look in your dressing-gown pocket.'

20

MOORED AT QUAYSIDE

The day after Rikki was admitted to Gartnavel Royal I went to visit and found him feeling utterly miserable. He hated being away from home and he didn't know why he was there. His face lit up when he saw me and he told me that he knew I would come to take him home. It was dreadful having to tell him that it couldn't be that day, and he retreated into his cocoon of misery. I tried very hard to cheer him up but it was no good. I had timed my visit to end when the evening meal was ready in the hope that having supper put before him would take his mind off being alone again. It wasn't much of a success. When we kissed good night Rikki was in tears. If he only knew how close I was to joining him!

I had walked over instead of driving, thinking some fresh air would be good for me, but as I got to the bottom of the hill I had to go up it didn't seem such a good idea. Then the rain came on and it was torrential. I wasn't wearing a raincoat and had nothing to cover my hair so in just a few moments I was soaked. With the rain running down my face I realised that no one could see if I was crying and with that freedom I cried myself home.

I went to see Rikki every day and on the third day I started to ask the staff when he could come home. Without exception they were all non-committal which I found disappointing.

What was uplifting, by contrast, was the kindness and

understanding we had from our friend, Tony Roper. Rikki and Tony had worked together for decades and were definitely on the same wavelength. With Tony and his beautiful wife Isobel we had some astoundingly happy meals in town, but the support they gave us during Rikki's ghastly illness was phenomenal. When Rikki had to go to Timbury House, Tony was a frequent visitor and how Rikki loved to see him. I had a lump in my throat sometimes when Tony was laughing loudly and so was Rikki. Tony was also the one who put me right on how long assessment takes, knowing it would be six or seven weeks.

It was incredibly hard to take the news that the result of the assessment was that Rikki could not be allowed to come home. The doctors and nurses were gentle and kind and they explained that Rikki was now so ill that he could be a danger to himself and he needed nursing-home care. All I had to do was find the right nursing home and I had no idea how to start.

I questioned the staff at Gartnavel and asked friends who had relatives being cared for in Glasgow which one they would recommend. At last I had it down to two, both run by BUPA, one in Yoker, the other in Clydebank. I made an appointment with the one in Yoker, called Quayside, as it was the nearer. How I could be so lucky I do not know. I had expected to spend considerable time viewing different homes, but the moment I walked through the door, met two of the office staff and then the manager, Mr Graham Kelly, that was it. Quayside was my choice.

Mr Kelly showed me round. There was a very nice open-plan sitting room which led off the dining room, and the feeling within the house was one of peace and space.

We had been lucky enough to arrive when there were two rooms available. I chose one for Rikki which had patio doors onto the garden. It had been cleverly constructed and looked like any other cared-for garden, but behind the bushes there were steel railings enclosing the whole area. This gave patients the run of the garden in safety. Mr Kelly told me that they would redecorate the bedroom to our chosen colours if we would like, but as the colours were very similar to our bedroom at home and looked very fresh there didn't seem much point in altering it. All the rooms were en suite, so patients had the choice of the communal area or their own privacy.

I told Mr Kelly I would very much like Rikki to come to Waverley House at Quayside, and would he and his staff please take care of him. It was arranged that he should move in three days later, on the Monday.

The Timbury staff could not have done more for Rikki, and I so admired their dedication and patience. They were real friends, but Timbury was a transitory place – Waverley House at Quayside was going to be permanent.

I took Rikki from Timbury to Quayside very nervously for I was afraid he would demand to go home, but he didn't. I wondered if someone suffering from Alzheimer's could become institutionalised after seven weeks, but I was delighted that Rikki and I were on our own and could enjoy the conversation and love we shared. He was made to feel most welcome when we arrived, and had no complaints at all about his room. These days he seemed to accept things much more easily, and I didn't know if that was the result of his illness or his medication. I tended to think it was the latter, but whatever the reason I was glad of it.

Another reason I had to be glad was that Quayside did the laundry! When Rikki was in Gartnavel I had to take it all home to wash and iron, which was perfectly all right and I wouldn't have expected it to be otherwise. The daily laundry was left in Rikki's room in a large plastic bag. I would take it home, and tip it straight into the washing machine. Then when the clothes were washed and I started to hang them up I couldn't count how many pairs of socks, vests and pants I discovered which neither Rikki nor I had ever seen before. I began to wonder if I had found my true vocation – laundry maid to the NHS . . .

I wondered if they were laundered well enough, but there were no letters of complaint!

Rikki was very upset when I had to leave him and so was I. I knew he would be feeling insecure again but I was sure the staff would understand and help him, and my goodness they did.

Graham (Mr Kelly, the staff and ourselves were now on first name terms) had asked about Rikki's interests and hobbies and I told him about his painting, now lapsed. He thought I should bring in his papers and paint to see if he might start again, which I did when I returned the next day.

I was met by my wonderful husband who was fired with enthusiasm to paint again. That was good but what was even better was the fact that Graham had booked Rikki into a weekly art class. It was held very near to Quayside and was designed for people with a disability. Rikki would walk round there with a nurse one morning a week and be brought back in time for lunch. What a happy arrangement! Rikki was so looking forward to it, and said he would start painting that very afternoon. To see him talking like that, smiling, and laughing, the way he used to, almost made me forget he had Alzheimer's. We couldn't stop hugging and kissing and laughing in the way we used to, and I had thought we never would again. I vowed I would treasure that morning and remember it for the rest of my life, and I do.

The next day I went to see him in the afternoon and bounced happily into his room to find a dejected Rikki who bore no resemblance to the man of the day before. I tried to get him to tell me what was wrong but he either couldn't or wouldn't. The staff had no idea either, but with that unspeakable illness there doesn't have to be a reason. I stayed for quite a long time and put out all the fruit and sweets I had brought Rikki, who had discovered that he had a sweet tooth. He had two large bowls, one filled with fresh fruit and the other with sweets, but that day he wasn't interested in either.

I thought I should go as I didn't think I was doing him any good. I kissed him goodbye and went out through the front door. I was walking towards the car park when heard my name being called and I turned round and saw Rikki. He had come through the garden from his room. I ran to him and suddenly we were together, on our own, just Rikki and me with a very high steel fence between us, but at least we could get our hands through the railings, so four hands were held and Rikki said, 'Take me with you, please Katie.'

If anyone had seen us what could they have thought? Two extremely upset elderly adults holding hands through a railing and crying their hearts out. That too was a moment I shall always remember, and that was two consecutive days.

I've come to the conclusion that the only thing you can depend on with Alzheimer's is that it is totally unpredictable.

Rikki was settling in remarkably well, and a pattern was emerging. He hated all the patients. He would have nothing to do with them. Not that that would worry any of them because they all lived in their own little worlds. The staff, on the other hand, he loved. There wasn't one member of staff he disliked, but he really loved Anne Marie who was in charge, and Dot, the nurse who looked after him like a mother. She knew all his moods, she teased him, and they would laugh together. In fact I thought it only fair to warn her that if I ever thought of divorcing Rikki she would be described as 'The Other Woman'. All the staff were just magical. The only trouble was that Rikki thought he was one of them! At the coffee breaks he would sit at their table and those dear people never sent him packing back to the patients. I'm sure that any contentment Rikki had was due to them.

Another lovely thing was that I was allowed to take Jake with me, and how Rikki and he enjoyed that. Tony was still a regular visitor and often he would take Jake for a walk in the garden, an exercise of which Jake highly approved. Jake's other delight was when he was given chocolate from the sweet bowl, something he never got at home. How he loved Quayside!

When Rikki and I were in his room we closed the door, but apart from that it was left open as were all the others, and as always outside in the corridor the Alzheimer Walk would go on. I wish I knew the reason for it, but if it's Alzheimer's who needs a reason?

One afternoon when Jake and I arrived, Rikki and Dot were deep in conversation in the sitting room so rather than disturb them I left Jake with them and went to put the fruit and sweets in their bowls. To my surprise the door was locked and I couldn't find a key anywhere. I would have to go back and ask Dot if she had one. I had only gone a few yards when Anne Marie appeared so I told her I couldn't get in to Rikki's room and she said, 'I must show you where we hide the key,' and she did. I was now curious to find out why the door was locked and Anne Marie told me that the endless patients in the Alzheimer Walk had all been going into his room to pinch the sweets. I thought about it and said to Anne Marie that I would just have to double the amount I was bringing.

'Don't even think of doing that, they're nearly all diabetic,' was the answer.

I had a phone call one day just as I was leaving for Quayside; it was Graham telling me that Rikki had been taken into the Western. It wasn't anything to worry about, a small operation, but he would need a general anaesthetic and be in for a day or two. I knew which operation it was, one that Rikki had every now and again, all I needed to know was when could I see him? The following morning should be all right, Graham thought, and I thanked him for letting me know.

Rikki was not happy in the Western. It was no fault of theirs, he was quite disorientated and desperately insecure. There were no familiar faces, but as often happened things got better. Rikki was in a little room which opened on to the ward and opposite him was a man who seemed heaven-sent. He and Rikki got on tremendously well and I'm sure he was responsible for Rikki's improved state of mind. He would go over and sit and talk to Rikki, which is exactly what he needed. I met his wife too, and we were able to compare notes. I think his name was Ian Russell; he gave me his business card so that I could send him and his wife a photograph of Rikki and I'm ashamed to say I mislaid it but recently found it, and at once phoned the firm, who were less than helpful. All they would say was that he no longer worked there and refused to give me any information to help me contact him. It will be on my conscience for the rest of my life!

It was quite an occasion when Rikki returned to Quayside. All the staff headed by Graham were there to welcome him back, and I'm told that all he could say was 'Thank God!'. He was so very glad to be back at what was now 'home'.

We were now happy to be together again, the three of us, and often, Tony.

Rikki seemed to be doing well but then he had a bad fall and broke his hip. It happened during the night when he fell out of bed and that was that. It was thought that he had been leaning over the side of the bed, and I'm sure that was correct. It's exactly what he did at home when he thought he had swallowed the keys. He would lean right out of the bed retching, in an attempt to dislodge them, but I was always there to haul him back and waken him up.

That fall made all the difference to him. He had to go back to the Western, where they put a metal plate in his hip. He never complained of pain, but he could no longer walk. That shattered everything. He couldn't remember words, he couldn't put sentences together, he didn't recognise people and now he couldn't move, and on top of all that he had that lethal bug MRSA. Things were bad and I didn't know what to do. All I wanted was to get him out of the hell he was in, but how?

It was now nearly Christmas time and one day as I was

leaving I met Graham. That wasn't unusual – he kept his finger on the pulse of Quayside, and he was wonderful at sharing time with Rikki. What did surprise me was that he asked if I would like Rikki to come home for Christmas. Wouldn't I just! But he wouldn't be returning to any hospital or nursing home after that. Rikki would come home and I would cook all his favourite things. We would have a celebration meal because we would be together and when we went to bed he would have his favourite brandy and Canada Dry but in it would be an extra ingredient which would mean he didn't wake up in the morning. He would be at peace. It would be so easy.

The following day when I went to see him I was told the infection had returned and he couldn't possibly go home.

Not being able to walk meant that Rikki was wheeled from his room to the sitting room in the morning and would be there for the day and that wasn't his idea of fun. Christmas Day couldn't have been worse for him. He could never stand being in a crowd, and naturally Quayside was bulging at the seams with all the relations and their families ranging from infants to rather sulky teenagers who obviously didn't want to be there. I imagined the conversation that had brought them: 'If you don't go and see your Grandmother at Christmas she'll cut you out of her will.'

In the middle of all the festive fun sat Rikki, not only miserable but angry. I was at a complete loss to know what to give him, then I remembered that our friends the Hoopers had given him a soft toy Westie from which he would not be parted. I had phoned Harrods and ordered their Christmas Bear and I also had bits and pieces, toiletries and chocolates, all of which he disliked. Then I produced the bear. I told Rikki that this poor little bear had nowhere to go at Christmas and was very lonely, and did he think he could give him a home?

I put the bear in Rikki's arms, he looked down at it and smiled, held it for some time, and then slowly raising his arm he flung it right across the room. I brought the bear home. He wears a red duffle, so I've called him Wuffle the Duffle, and he sits in the drawing room in Rikki's chair with a book of his press cuttings so that he can read about the man who nearly owned him!

Things did improve for Rikki when we were into January. He seemed a little calmer but the wretched infection was doing its worst and I don't think that he had recovered from Christmas. I had found out why he was so angry then; it wasn't only the noise and crowd that upset him, it was because Dot was dressed as Mother Christmas and he didn't recognise her. He kept looking for his favourite nurse but couldn't find her. All was well when she returned in her uniform!

I had quite a traumatic time myself before Christmas. I had looked forward to seeing the pantomime at the King's, starring Elaine C. Smith and Gerard Kelly, and it was a tremendous success. I went with a friend and neighbour, Anna di Mascio, on the first night and we enjoyed it thoroughly. During the second half I gradually had the strangest sensation and I didn't feel very well! I had to keep that information to myself as I was sitting next to the Chief Executive of the King's, the charming David Williams, and I certainly didn't want him, or anyone else, to think I wasn't enjoying myself. In our taxi on the way home I told Anna how I felt and she was most sympathetic, so instead of us having a final glass of wine I went to bed and Anna went home.

Fortunately for me Anna had my house keys – that's because her super husband Romi takes Jake for a walk twice a day – so on Saturday morning she let herself in, and came up to the bedroom to see how I was. She soon found out how I was – unconscious! She phoned a neighbour who is a doctor then she phoned Doreen, my sister, and when the doctor took one look at me she phoned for an ambulance. I was blissfully unaware of the busy morning they were having. When the ambulance arrived Doreen and I were taken to the Western Infirmary. Not surprisingly they didn't like the look of me at all, so we were sent to the Southern General Hospital. There I was admitted for Emergency Brain Surgery. I only learned about this when I was recovering from the operation. I assumed if it was brain surgery, they were trying to find out if I had one . . .

It seems I had two subdural haematomas. It's amazing what you can have without knowing about it. In everyday language it means clot. It's quite sensible really – how very much quicker and easier it is to call someone 'you clot' rather than 'you subdural haematoma'.

Recovery took time, and it was so difficult not being able to see Rikki as much as I would have liked but I suppose I was lucky to be alive.

One of the saddest things to happen around this time was when I arrived with Jake to visit Rikki. Although Rikki welcomed me he ignored Jake. When we were both sitting down and talking together, little Jake, who I think was feeling neglected, went to Rikki and very gently pawed his leg. Rikki's only reaction was a frown. After some minutes Jake tried again, but this time Rikki was really annoyed and said sternly to me, 'Who is that?'

I thought he was joking, but I just said with a smile 'It's Jake, darling,' but Rikki shook his head, 'That's not Jake, it's nothing like Jake.' And that was that, I never took him back to Quayside. I think it was then that I realised how very ill Rikki was. To be unable to recognise the dog he had loved for years was so terribly sad. Nonetheless I know how lucky I was, because Rikki and I had no problem with recognising each other. Nor did we have any problem with talking. Anyone listening to us would probably think we were speaking a foreign language!

My greatest fear was that there might come a time when he wouldn't know me, and we could never be close again. But we didn't have that problem.

Shortly after Jake's dismissal I had a phone call from Quayside to say that Rikki wasn't well and they had sent for the doctor. I went straight there and was in time to see my doctor, Helen, before she left, looking very thoughtful and she told me that the MRSA bug had returned with a vengeance and was making him very ill. It seemed to me that Rikki shouldn't be left alone, and the nursing home allowed me to stay with him through the night. I sat in a chair beside his bed, which meant that I could hold his hand, make soothing noises when he had nightmares, and most of all make sure he didn't fall out of bed. I liked looking after him again, it seemed so right. When the nurses came to waken him in the morning I went home to sleep before I returned to Quayside in the evening.

It was a good arrangement and Doreen, always a tower of strength in an emergency, looked after Jake. He couldn't believe his luck. He'd never had so many walks in one day nor such long ones!

Rikki seemed to be getting weaker, but he never complained or said he was in pain.

One morning I kissed him goodbye as usual, and went home to get some sleep. About noon I had a phone call to say that Rikki's condition was giving the nurses cause for concern. They had sent for Helen, and suggested I might like to go too.

When I got there Helen had already given him something to help him relax, and he was peaceful and sleepy, a good combination. She said she would come back in the evening and Rikki should have a restful afternoon. This he did, being cared for by his special friend, Dot. I was glad it was her, and although we didn't talk much we shared the same feeling. Dot didn't say anything specific, but something about her attitude and her sad face made me ask her how long she thought Rikki would live.

'For a few hours,' she said.

I expected to feel numb when I heard that, but I didn't. On the contrary, it was as though all my senses had been heightened. I knew Dot was about to go off duty. She left the room and returned with her coat on, said a quick goodbye, and went over to Rikki, where she stood looking down at him. Then she leant over, kissed the top of his forehead, and quickly went away. Behind her she left Rikki sleeping peacefully, quite unaware that his face was covered in her tears.

His room was busy with nurses all of that late afternoon, and in the early evening Helen came back. Thankfully no one came out with a comforting cliché, everything was matter-of-fact. At around seven the nurses left, there was nothing more they could do, but they said I only had to call or press the buzzer and they would be there in seconds, and I knew they meant it.

For now, though, it seemed so right that Rikki and I were alone together. I had no idea what to expect, but whatever it was, all that mattered was that we should share his last moments together. He was looking positively serene, and being Rikki, I guessed he'd decided what his death scene would be. I just had to wait for it.

Around eight o'clock his breathing slowed and became more shallow. I thought he hadn't long to live, and I was determined not to waste our last seconds together. I knew that the one sense that remains is the power of hearing, so for the next five minutes I quite loudly and clearly told Rikki how much I loved him and always would. I reminded him of the joys and laughter we had shared, and thanked him for our love, then I kissed him and sat back. There was a slight rustling sound, and Rikki's head came slowly off the pillow and he kissed me firmly on the mouth then laid his head back on the pillow and stopped breathing.

I sat there for a few minutes holding his hand then I gently closed his beautiful but sightless eyes, knowing it was the last time we could ever touch each other. I left the room to tell the nurses that Rikki had died at 8.20pm.

227

21

FINALE

I had promised to phone Tony, who knew how imminent Rikki's death was, whenever it happened. Though he knew it was inevitable, all he seemed concerned about was how I was going to get home. I told him I would get a taxi, but Tony wouldn't hear of it, insisting he would drive me home. I tried to dissuade him because he lives on the outskirts of Glasgow in the opposite direction, but at the same time the thought of going back to the house with a friend seemed a lovely idea. As usual he ignored my protests and said he would leave at once.

While I was waiting I talked to the nurses, and asked where Rikki would be taken. They told me that the undertakers Jonathan Harvey would soon be coming for him but if I wanted to use another firm he could be taken there the next day. Left to my own devices I would automatically have gone back to Wyllie and Lochhead, but if Quayside worked with Jonathan Harvey that was good enough for Rikki and me.

It seemed in no time Tony was there, and he had excelled himself in bringing his wife Isobel with him. It was so good to see her and the three of us had a great hugging session. There were no tears, just the panacea of three people who loved Rikki and now could share their feelings. On our journey home we were sharing them so much we missed a turning and became completely lost! When we found our way and got home I was so glad Tony and Isobel were with me. The house would have seemed very bleak, and although I knew I could have handled it, how much nicer it was to come in with friends. We sat and talked for ages, and drank a toast to Rikki. When Tony and Isobel left I realised that I hadn't had any sleep since Monday morning and it was now dawn on Wednesday. I went to bed and slept soundly.

In the morning my first phone call was to Jonathan Harvey to ask if they would be Rikki's undertakers. They agreed they would, and that one of their company would call on me that day. The 'one' turned out to be their manager Ewan Henderson. He was a gift from the Gods! I don't know anyone who could have coped with the slightly unusual funeral I was looking for as well as he did.

He came to see me the next day and after he had been talking for quite a short time I knew this was someone I could trust. There can't be anything he doesn't know about funerals, and far from disapproving of what I wanted, he liked it. Basically what I was looking for was a real celebration of Rikki's life. Of course there would be a few prayers and hymns, but other than that I knew that Rikki would want the congregation to be entertained. Rikki always liked colour, so I mentioned in his death notice that black ties were not necessary. Then I contacted all the friends and relatives that I could and begged them not to wear black.

Ewan very wisely suggested we should book the last available time at the crematorium, which would mean I could shake hands with everyone as they left, knowing we were not holding up another funeral party. The next thing was finding a place for the wake. We looked at a few hotels but it wasn't until we went to the Glasgow Hilton that we found just what we were looking for. The manager of functions was most helpful even though he was just about to go on holiday and it was his assistant who would be looking after us. She too was charming and excellent. In a very short time we chose the menu for the buffet meal and ordered the drinks and wines, said thank you, and left. How easy life becomes when you're with someone who knows what they are doing!

My next appointment was one I was dreading, registering Rikki's death. For that I had to go to Martha Street. I'd only been there once before and that was to get married. I once looked at Rikki's diary entry for our wedding day, to see how romantically he had described it, and there it was! 'Martha Street 3.15pm.' The reason I was dreading this was because I had none of the documents which were needed. The week before he went into Gartnavel Rikki decided to clean out his study and that involved hours of shredding. Only after he died did I realise he must have included our birth certificates and marriage certificates in the shredder. I was at the mercy of the registrar. Thankfully she was most merciful and managed to have duplicate papers made, and the problem was solved.

The next thing on my agenda was to phone as many friends as possible and here I made a dreadful mistake. I only spoke to friends in Scotland and of all people I forgot Rikki's long-lost friend, Leslie Bond, who lives in Godalming in England. I'm afraid my thoughts over the next days were greatly centred on Glasgow. It was a while before I realised my omission, and phoned right away. Leslie happened to be visiting his family in Australia, though his wife did say that if I had told him he would almost certainly have come to the funeral. I wore sackcloth and ashes for days!

I was trying very hard to plan things as Rikki would have liked, and one thing he had said over and over again was, 'If I ever leave this house it will be feet first.' I phoned Ewan and asked if Rikki could be brought home on the Monday night so that he would go to the crematorium from his own home. As I had hoped Ewan couldn't have been more accommodating, and he guaranteed that on Tuesday morning it would be feet first. I suggested that probably the evening would be the best time as it would be dark and I thought it better that people didn't see the coffin being brought out. I was afraid it might upset the neighbours who had known him so long. Things didn't quite work out that way. The hearse came slowly and silently around the corner just as Ewan had promised but what neither of us had expected were the two traffic policemen on their bikes with lights flashing, escorting him!

The police were magnificent. Rikki knew and liked 'the Boys' in the traffic police and had done a lot of charity work with them and loved every minute of it. They were commanded by Sergeant Steve Macnally, who is a splendid guy. When it was suggested that Rikki's escort should be from the Clydebank Police who are responsible for policing the crematorium, Steve would have none of it. Rikki would be seen off by *his* boys and what a beautiful job they made of it. I hope Steve and his senior officer were proud of them.

On the Monday night Rikki was left to rest in the dining room and the coffin was open; he looked as though he was having a welcome and peaceful sleep. I had told Ewan about the clown make-up my father had been given and I was sure nothing like that was going to happen this time and of course it didn't. All I can say is that Rikki looked like Rikki, and what more could I ask? There were quite a lot of friends around that night, just looking in for a moment, but nothing was planned except for my very good friend, Anne Doogan, who had travelled down from Aberdeen to stay with me. I was so glad to see her. Naturally I had quite a few drinks to pour and we kept the drinks cabinet in the dining room! Each time I went in I apologised to Rikki for disturbing him but he didn't seem to mind, though I was concerned when someone asked for a brandy and Canada Dry because that was Rikki's drink. My apology was profound that time.

On Tuesday morning Ewan and his team arrived. They gave me time for a last farewell, and I kissed Rikki's face for the final time, then they came in to close the coffin. He was carried, as he had decreed, feet first, out of the house and into the hearse. It had poured with rain all day but as we went down the front steps it stopped for just a moment.

The silver hearse drew slowly away and we followed in the first silver car. Originally I intended to wear a silver-grey suit and it's just as well I chose something else or they would never have managed to find me! As we turned the corner I saw some neighbours having a conversation, but they stopped when the hearse passed them and then we turned into Great Western Road to discover people lining the pavement and waving to Rikki's coffin. When we got the length of Anniesland every junction at the cross was crowded with people who started to applaud whenever the hearse came into view and until it was out of sight. It was so totally unexpected and one of the most moving things I have ever witnessed. I desperately wanted to cry, but that would have let the side down! Instead I waved back and smiled my thanks.

I thought how typical of the people of Glasgow that they would come out on a cold wet February day to say goodbye to someone they obviously cared for. I told my friends in the car that I was in bits, and we hadn't even reached the crematorium yet. There were people scattered all the way to Clydebank and large crowds at all the traffic lights, and even they had been fixed! Each and everyone of them was at green and we never stopped once. I think our traffic department is the best in the world.

We arrived at North Dalnottar crematorium to find another crowd braving the weather; they were the ones who couldn't get seats but were staying outside to hear the service broadcast to them.

It was so good to see Alastair; he made me feel confident. If the Reverend Alastair Symington was in control what could go wrong, especially as he was resplendent in his robes of Chaplain to Her Majesty the Queen. Ewan had given me the single red rose I had asked for, and now Alastair took it from me and placed it on Rikki's coffin. He said a short prayer and gave some readings from the Bible then he asked Mr Tony Roper to give the eulogy.

Mr Roper did and what a eulogy it was! The congregation seemed a little startled at first, and there was a slight feeling of 'Is it all right to laugh in Church?' but the way Tony was speaking left them no option. He was at his brilliant best, the congregation was now more of an audience, and Tony had us all in the palm of his hand. Not only did he get all the laughs he got a round of applause with one, and then another at his finale. There was a slight vocal interruption from the gallery at one point and Tony stopped in mid-sentence, stared at the coffin and said, 'Is that you Rikki?' The audience loved that.

He came back to sit down feeling, I hope, that it was a job well done. Tony sat on my right and dear Billy Differ was on my left. They were there for a purpose and they were being very gallant. My spine has twisted, probably because of the arthritis I've had for several years, and my balance can be non-existent. Tony and Billy were going to support me at the moment in the service where we all had to stand, otherwise I would have fallen flat on my face! It's a habit I've got used to – in fact I had a rather bad fall two days before the funeral and the dark glasses I wore were not to hide tears but two black eyes!

Tony's act was followed by another. This time it was dear Alasdair Gillies, who beautifully sang 'Ae Fond Kiss'. It was a very wet day but as he sang the rain stopped and a bright shaft of sunlight came through the window and rested on the coffin. It was then I knew. Rikki was directing the lighting!

Now it was time for the ace up my sleeve. We sang a hymn and then Alastair Symington began his sermon. There was a feeling of everyone straightening their faces but they needn't have bothered. In a very few minutes he had them roaring with laughter again. Alastair is an outstanding after-dinner speaker and his wit is well known. He had twenty years of close friendship with Rikki to draw on, which he did. After a memorable performance Alastair ended his sermon and introduced a hymn.

Shortly after Rikki died Tony and I had had a conversation. Tony had phoned me, but I was feeling very down that day and Tony was being so very kind that I had to say to him,

'Tony, please don't be so nice to me – it'll make me cry.'

'You stupid bitch!' he said.

I could only reply, 'Oh thank you, Tony, that's much better.'

Back at the funeral service Alastair asked everyone to stand and Tony and Billy helped me to my feet and held my arms. This, the commital, was something I was afraid of. I had so often teased Rikki that when he died I would take him to North Dalnottar to be cremated, because I knew that when the curtains closed he wouldn't be able to resist taking a call. It had seemed funny at the time, but not now. As the curtains began to close very, very, slowly I could feel the tears gathering. Not now, I thought, please, not now. I pressed Tony's arm.

'Call me a bitch,' I whispered.

'You *are* a bitch,' he whispered back.

'Thank you.' So I didn't cry. I'm not sure why, but I felt I would be letting Rikki down if I did. The going-out music was a favourite of his – 'Style' sung by his favourite singer, Frank Sinatra. I think Rikki used that number in practically every pantomime he wrote and directed. It seemed appropriate. I hope he enjoyed it.

Tony and Billy hovered as I shook hands with everyone but I was able to get my back against the door jamb which helped enormously. It was most touching to see who had come – colleagues, friends and fans, and I was especially pleased to see how many of the people who had nursed Rikki came, people to whom I owe a great debt of gratitude. I'm happy to say that Graham Kelly, Anne Marie and, bless her, Dot were among them.

Ron Bain who had been such a help at the crematorium had gone to the Hilton to get things started. The shaking of hands took quite a time and the last thing I wanted was to have my guests waiting for me.

When I did get there I walked into a room full of friends. A lovely feeling.

Perhaps Rikki's range of friends was summed up by one day just after he died. In the morning a beautiful bouquet of flowers arrived from the Lord Provost, Liz Cameron, with a card which said, 'In memory of Scotland's favourite entertainer.' And in the afternoon a lovely card came through the door, signed, 'With deepest sympathy, the bin men.' Rikki liked them all so much and he always had a chat when he met them while walking Jake. It says it all, doesn't it?

After Rikki's funeral I had a heart-warming letter from Gregor Fisher. He began, 'I'm not sure if it's correct and proper to say how much I enjoyed the celebration of Rikki's life,' and ended, 'I'll miss him, but weren't we lucky to have known him, and be able to bask in the sunshine of the laughter he gave us.'

I was determined not to cry at Rikki's funeral and I didn't, but when I came to writing about it the tears just wouldn't stop. I remember how deeply disappointed I was when I came home from the Hilton. I was convinced Rikki would be there, but he wasn't of course, not the next day nor the next.

I sat and thought for a long time, then thinking of Rikki's excellent good manners I realised that I hadn't invited him to come home. So I did, and he's been here ever since. I'm still completely in love with him and that brings a form of freedom with it, because basically I want to be with him, and if I became ill and was told it was terminal, I would be very glad. That sounds ungrateful, as I have so many wonderful friends and my sister and her family, all of whom I love dearly. But I want to belong to Rikki again, and that gives me a sense of detachment. That can be very useful, it means I can't be hurt.

I have settled with the thought that I shall be with Rikki again, but what if there is no afterlife? I certainly don't know, but neither the ministers, the Archbishops nor the Pope *know*. They all *believe*, which is quite different. One way or another I definitely will be with him. I have Rikki's ashes at home here, and when it's my turn for cremation, I have left instructions that our ashes should be mingled in the same casket with our two wedding rings placed on them. At the moment I wear both of them. If I can't be with him spiritually, then I will be with him physically, and that's better than nothing!

How am I aware that Rikki is here? He finds things for me, but only if I ask him.

Some years ago I bought a pair of men's gilt armbands because I like to push the sleeves of sweaters up my forearm and if they won't stay that way I use my armbands. Some weeks ago I mislaid them. I knew they were in the house, but though I searched everywhere I couldn't find them. Last week I went to Tesco and as I left the house I said, 'Darling, I've hunted everywhere for my armbands but I can't find them, could you have a look?'

When I got back I put the groceries in our large walk-in store cupboard in the scullery. Next morning I thought I would have some of that porridge that you microwave and I was opening the packet I had bought the day before when I noticed an already opened box behind it. I could hear my sister's voice ringing in my ears, 'Finish that one before you open a new one.' Obediently I took the older box down to discover my armbands behind it. Now who would think of looking for armbands behind the porridge? That's always the way it works. There's a 24 hour wait and then, the find.

One morning I was chatting to Paul at the surgery and I told him of Rikki's brilliance at finding things. He said, 'I wish he would find my pen for me.' I said I would ask him. I knew how much the pen meant to Paul. He had been given it by a pop group after one member who was losing his voice was treated by Paul with great success. They had had it engraved for him, but he had lost it for weeks. That afternoon he phoned me and said, 'You're not going to believe this.' 'Try me,' I replied.

Later that morning Paul had gone to see another doctor to discuss some project or other. They had been at University together and enjoyed their meetings.

When Paul arrived his friend opened a drawer, and said, 'Paul, I've got something for you,' and took out a packet of biscuits saying, 'I bought some of these last week, and they were so good I got you some.'

Paul's face fell. 'That's kind of you, but I hoped it might be my pen.'

His friend shook his head, 'No, your pen's on the desk where you left it last time you were here.'

So now it's not just me who believes Rikki is here, Paul does too – and you can trust him, he's a doctor!

RIKKI FULTON'S
THE REV I.M. JOLLY

HOW I FOUND GOD
AND WHY HE WAS HIDING FROM ME

by Tony Roper

Book One of the hilarious adventures
of Scotland's best-loved minister

The Reverend I.M. Jolly always has a few wee problems,
but life goes from bad to worse when he finds out he may
soon be out of a job, thinks his beloved wife Ephesia is
having an affair and that his parishoners want rid of him.
It's enough to wipe the smile off his face . . .

Also available on 4-cassette audio tape,
read by Tony Roper

RIKKI FULTON'S
THE REV I.M. JOLLY

ONE DEITY AT A TIME,
SWEET JESUS

by Tony Roper

*Book Two of the hilarious adventures
of Scotland's best-loved minister*

Just when you thought it was safe to go to church again,
he's back! And now he's in residence at Balmoral – you
can tell because the flag's at half-mast. But when Jolly is
sent off on a secret mission, anything could happen. Jolly's
back. And this time he means business.